Quilt Block
Leftovers

Quilt Block
Leftovers

CLEVER USES FOR SPARE SQUARES

Sarah Phillips

Sterling Publishing Co., Inc.
New York

PROLIFIC IMPRESSIONS PRODUCTION STAFF:

Editor in Chief: **MICKEY BASKETT**

Creative Director: **JOEL TRESSLER**

Photography: **JOEL TRESSLER**

Graphics: **ALLYSON FRYE**

Administration: **JIM BASKETT**

10 9 8 7 6 5 4 3 2 1

Published by Sterling Publishing Co., Inc.
387 Park Avenue South, New York, N.Y. 10016

© 2005 by Prolific Impressions, Inc.

Produced by Prolific Impressions, Inc.
160 South Candler St., Decatur, GA 30030

Distributed in Canada by Sterling Publishing
c/o Canadian Manda Group, One Atlantic Avenue, Suite 105
Toronto, Ontario, Canada M6K 3E7
Distributed in Great Britain by Chrysalis Books Group PLC,
The Chrysalis Building, Bramley Road, London W10 6SP, England
Distributed in Australia by Capricorn Link (Australia) Pty. Ltd.
P.O. Box 704, Windsor, NSW 2756 Australia

Printed in China
All rights reserved
For information about custom editions, special sales, premium and corporate purchases, please contact Sterling Special Sales Department at 800-805-5489 or specialsales@sterlingpub.com
Bookspan ISBN-13: 978-1-4027-3782-4
          ISBN-10:   1-4027-3782-3

Contents

102

57

23

Sarah Phillips grew up in the Atlanta area and learned to sew as a child during her summers with her great aunt in California. She discovered quilting in 1995 when she was pregnant with her second child. Her son wanted his little sister's new quilt and became very excited when he found out he would have the opportunity to pick all his own fabric if his mom made him a quilt.

From that first quilt, Sarah grew to love the art of quilting and eventually turned her passion into a business that she now owns in Atlanta, Georgia, called Intown Quilters.

She tries hard to supply all the local quilters with unusual 100% cotton quilting fabric from places around the world like Bali, Malaysia, Australia, Africa, and Japan, and has always got her eye out for wonderful new fabric.

Sarah finds it very satisfying helping fellow quilters pick out fabric, figure out the yardage for projects and locate that infamous piece of fabric, notion, book or pattern that seems impossible to find.

Sarah lives about 3 miles from her shop in Decatur, Georgia with her husband Richard Kahn, their two children Hana and Zachary, their three cats and a dog.

THANKS...

Pat Kilmark, Carol Homrich, Peggy Delmar, Vicky Clark, Michael Dean and Annette Florence for providing blocks used in these projects.

Tan Trammell, Arlene Poretsky, Patty Murphy, Carol Jaynes, Sheila Blair, Joan Wiezenthal and Shannon Baker--all of you worked tirelessly contributing projects. Joel Tressler--for giving me this opportunity.

My wonderful employees and friends for all their support to me, my shop and this book!

My mother Jane Phillips for her help with editing and her moral support, my brother Michael Phillips for saying "...you're crazy if you don't do it," as well as all his never-ending support to me, my shop and my family. Sue Kahn--mother-in-law extraordinaire.

Ansley and Emma Murphey, Kate LaRocco, Kyle and Lucky Tressler and Kinsley Driscol for their modeling talents.

Finally, and most importantly, I would like to thank my husband Richard Kahn and my children Hana and Zachary Kahn for loving and supporting me through the long hours I have had to put into my shop, writing, and sewing for this book.

Introduction

Do you just love your hobby of quilting? Do you wish you had more time to get more projects done? Well, this book will provide you with quick easy projects to make with just one or a few quilt blocks. You will be able to create projects for your home or gifts for others that will add your quilting creativity to your home decorations and to all your gift giving. The projects in this book are perfect for those extra blocks you have just lying around or, with the patterns provided, you can make a quilt block just for a specific project.

When you think of quilting do you think of countless hours sitting with scissors, needle and thread? Have you been interested in quilting, but thought that you did not have the time or the patience to take it up?

Quilting is basically stitches holding together two pieces of fabric with a piece of fill (batting, interfacing, flannel) inside. The stitches secure the three layers together so that the finished piece will hold up to wear. This can be done by hand or machine with many different types of thread. Machine quilting can be done at home on a traditional sewing machine or on a long-arm machine by a professional long-arm quilter. There are even a growing number of "quilters" who are investing in long-arm quilting machines for their own personal use so that they can have their quilts machine quilted quickly, but do it themselves.

Quilting really is an enjoyable art form that can fill the need for creativity for many who have believed themselves void of creativity in the past. It is a great craft for people who have problems drawing and are good with the mathematical side

of their brains because the true secret to a smooth quilt top is accurate mathematical calculations (just basic adding, subtracting, multiplying, and dividing) along with accurate cutting and a consistent $1/4''$ seam. Don't let the math scare you non-mathematical people away. It is not hard math. The point here is that quilting can work for any and every person. You don't have to be a great artist to be able to quilt. You don't even have to be a great sewer to be a quilter. The sewing for quilting is far more straight forward and easy than sewing for apparel or home decorating.

Quilting really is satisfying as an art-form and you should try if you have been thinking about it!!!

General Quilting Supplies

Quilting can be accomplished with as little as a pair of scissors, a needle, fabric and batting. Many quilts have been made this way and there are still a few quilters who will tell you that it is the only true way.

In the last 10-15 years, however, there have been great developments in the quilting tool world. There are many new tools that not only make quilting much easier, but also make it much more fun.

I believe that you must have a rotary cutter, a cutting mat and a 24″ long ruler to be successful enough to want to keep quilting.

Fabric

In traditional quilting, 100% cotton fabric is generally used. It comes in 42″- 45″ widths. It is always good to pre-shrink the cloth before using to avoid problems in the finished project.

Rotary Cutter and Mat

It is best to cut your fabric for quilting with a rotary cutter for straight accurate piecing. For rotary cutting you will need a cutting mat at least 18″ x 24″ and a 6″ x 24″ clear acrylic ruler. There are many other size rulers you may choose to have, but you really need to have a 24″ long ruler that is 6″ - 8″ wide.

Rotary cutters are a dangerous tool. It is very important to keep the safety lock on at all times and only release it when you are cutting. Make sure you get in the practice of always keeping the safety lock on when you are not using the rotary cutter.

Rulers

You will need rulers to use with your rotary cutter and cutting mat.There are many different size rulers available, but I think it is best to have a 6″ x 24″ clear acrylic ruler. Clear rulers are helpful so that you can see where the fabric truly is under the ruler.

Scissors

You will need both paper and fabric scissors. The paper for pattern cutting and the fabric scissors for cloth. It is also helpful to have a small pair or scissors for cutting threads.

Marking Tools

When using fabric in piecing, it is often necessary to mark cutting or stitching lines onto the cloth. There are many types of marking tools such as pencils, chalk wheels, wash-away pens, air-erase pens, and iron-away marking tools. They come in many different colors. You will need to test several and pick the ones that work best for you.

General Quilting Supplies

Needles

The most commonly used needles for piecing are Sharps in assorted sizes. For quilting, Betweens are used in sizes 8 to 12. The higher the number on the package of needles, the smaller the size of the needle.

There are several sizes of machine needles that you may want to have on hand for piecing and quilting. The basic needle needed for machine-piecing is usually 80/12. You might want to have a 90/14 for heavier fabrics and a top-stitch 100/16 for heavier threads. There are also special metallic needles for use with metallic threads.

Thread

It is usually good to sew with a thread of the same fiber content as the cloth being used. In piecing 100% cotton sewing thread is best. In quilting 100% cotton hand-quilting thread is best for quilting by hand. Synthetic threads are often used for decorative machine quilting and embellishment.

Sewing Machine

There are many types of sewing machines available on the market. It is best to try out several different types and prices of machines and pick the one that is easiest to figure out how to use.

Quilting Hoop

A quilting hoop is used to stabilize a project for hand-quilting.

Thimble

It is helpful to use a thimble on the middle finger when piecing or quilting by hand. There are many different types of thimbles so it is best to try many and find the one that is most comfortable on your finger.

Pins

It is important to use straight-pins when piecing so you have accurate seams and points.

When pin-basting for quilting, it is nice to use curved safety pins to baste with. They are easier to put through the three layers of the project and they help to keep the layers from moving while putting them in.

Seam Ripper

It does not matter how careful we are, there will always be a seam that needs to be torn out. Make sure you have a good seam ripper to make this job easier.

GENERAL QUILTING INSTRUCTIONS:
Preparing your fabric for quilting

Pre-wash all your fabric to remove excess dye, sizing and to pre-shrink your fabric. Machine-wash on delicate in warm water, dry on warm setting with a clean dry towel in the dryer, checking every 5 minutes to see if it is dry. You can check a swatch of fabric in a clear container of water to test for colorfastness or you can just play it safe and wash all fabric with a dye setting product.

Rotary Cutting

One of the greatest advances made in sewing and quilting has been the rotary cutter used along with a cutting mat and ruler. When cutting fabric with a rotary cutter, you push the cutter away from your body along the edge of the ruler to get straight edges on your pieces. Only push the cutter one time and be sure to put enough pressure on it to cut through all the layers of fabric. If there is a part of the cut that did not go all the way through, carefully and very slowly cut just that

The blade runs next to the ruler when using a rotary cutter. This ensures a nice clean cut.

part again or use scissors to cut it apart. It is very easy to make the edge messy if you run the cutter over a cut several times. When you measure and cut accurately you will get a smoother finished project.

Pressing

Pressing fabric for quilting is done differently than pressing clothing. It is best to press parallel to the selvedge and placing the iron down on top of the fabric making sure not to push back and forth over the fabric to avoid stretching of the fabric. Seams should be pressed flat, while still folded right-sides together, and then pressed to one side, usually toward the dark fabric, unless a pattern calls for pressing the seams open (some piecing lays flatter if the seams are pressed open).

Be sure to keep fingers away from the edge of the ruler when using a rotary cutter.

General Instructions

Using Templates

You can copy templates from a pattern or a book by laying transparent plastic template material over the printed template pattern and tracing with a fine-point permanent marker. Trace and cut out on the stitching line (broken line) for hand piecing templates or cut on the outer solid line for machine piecing templates. Make sure to label each template. Poke a tiny hole at each seam crossing point for matching up where you will start your seams.

Hand Piecing

When you cut your pieces for hand piecing make sure to draw your $1/4''$ seam allowance on all your pieces to ensure straight accurate seams. Place 2 fabric pieces right sides together. Match corners or other seam crossing points to align seams and pin together. Use a single strand of quality cotton sewing thread about 18″ long and a sharps needle of your choice. To secure thread, begin at a match point and without a knot, take a stitch and a backstitch on the seam-line. Make smooth running stitches, closely and evenly spaced, stitching on the drawn line on both patches of fabric. Backstitch at the end of the seam-line. Do not stitch into the seam allowances. Press seams after the block is completed. To join the seamed pieces and strengthen the intersection, stitch through the seam allowances and backstitch directly before and immediately after them.

Machine Piecing

Use a $1/4''$ machine foot to guide your fabric or place a strip of masking tape or moleskin on the machine throat plate $1/4''$ from the needle position (it is best to try to get a $1/4''$ foot for your machine). Place 2 fabric pieces right- sides and raw-edges together and pin (with the pin going into the fabric from the raw-edge side straight across the seam-line).

Begin and end stitching at the raw edges without backstitching. Make sure the thread tension and stitches are smooth and even on both sides of the seam. When sewing seamed pieces together, line up seams and pin right at the seam to make sure that your points match. Press each seam before going on to the next. If you are making many of one type of unit, you can feed your pinned pieces under the needle one right after the other without cutting any threads in between. When you are done piecing all you want at one time you can cut all threads between the units and press them open. This method is called strip-piecing.

Paper Piecing

When paper-piecing the printed side of the paper is the back of the block, so your blocks will always be the reverse of the image you see. The pattern pieces are numbered to distinguish the order in which these pieces are sewn onto the paper. The numbers need to be followed in order. It is helpful to cut out your pieces quite a bit larger than needed because it is very easy to end up without your points/corners covered. It is important to rip the paper off the back of the block very carefully so as not to rip any of the stitch out. It is easier to rip the paper off the back if you copy your pattern onto very thin paper like the newsprint type of paper found in inexpensive kids' coloring pads or the thinnest printing paper. You can also make the paper easier to rip off by using a very small stitch length and by folding the paper where the stitches are back and forth to weaken the paper at the stitch point.

Paper-piecing can be a bit confusing the first few times you do it, but after you have practiced it, you will find it a great tool for getting very precise points. I recommend taking a class on it if possible because teachers can give many tips for making it easier. If paper-piecing frustrates you the first few times you try it. Keep trying!

General Instructions

Mark a line at a 45 degree angle then sew along the line to make a mitered corner.

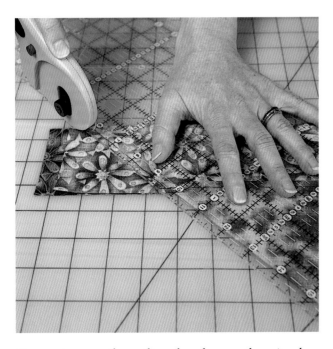

Be sure to open the quilt and make sure the miter lays flat before cutting off the excess.

Mitering Corners

Some quilt top designs and certain fabrics (where the pattern needs to be matched up) look better if the border is mitered. Mitering the border means sewing an angled seam at the corners rather than sewing borders onto two sides of a quilt top and then onto the other two sides overlapping the first two borders. Cut border strips the finished length and width of the quilt plus 4″ to 6″ extra in order to miter them.

Pin the border strips to the quilt top so that you have the same amount overhanging on each end. Start stitching the borders a $^1/_4$″ from the beginning of the top and finish the stitches a $^1/_4$″ from the end making sure to backstitch these seams. Press the seams toward the quilt top, away from the border. Lay quilt top right side up on ironing board fold quilt on a diagonal, right sides together. Line up the border strips' raw edges and the points where the seams end and pin in place. Mark a line from the end of the seams out to the edge of the borders in a 45° angle. Stitch along marked line backstitching at the beginning. About 1 inch from the end of the seam stop and make the stitch length smaller. Press seam to one side carefully so you do not stretch the border at the bias seam. Lay the quilt right side up check to make sure of the 45° angle seam with an acrylic ruler that has a 45° angle printed on it. If the seam is correct and the corner is flat, trim the $^1/_4$″ seam allowance.

If you choose to have more than one mitered border, sew border strips together first and then attach to the quilt top as one unit.

Marking Quilting Patterns

Press quilt top before marking only and do not press again until markings are removed, as many markings can be made permanent by pressing. Choose a tool which makes a thin accurate line and pre-test to make sure that it comes out in the method it claims to on quilt fabric scraps (see below for types of marking tools). Each project you encounter may take more than one marking tool depending on the color and type of fabric you are using.

Marking tool options include:
- A. Water soluble
- B. Air erasable markers
- C. Dressmaker's chalk
- D. Chalk pencils
- E. Chalk rolling markers
- F. Slivers of hardened soap
- G. Iron-away marking tools

Useful tools for using with marking tools are freezer paper, stencils, templates, and many household items such as cookie cutters, plates, jars, etc. and acrylic rulers.

Backing

Use the same quality backing fabric as used in the quilt top. Remove selvages and cut backing at least 4″ larger than quilt top on all sides. You will need your backing to be at least 10″ bigger on one end and 6″ bigger on the other end of the quilt if you are going to have it quilted by a long-arm quilter. It is necessary to seam backing for quilts larger than 36″ wide when using standard 40″- 42″ wide fabric. You can use either vertical or horizontal seaming, whichever requires less fabric, although many quilters feel that vertical seaming should always be used and that the back should never be seamed in the middle either horizontally or vertically. To avoid having seams in the middle of the backing you can split the second piece into two lengths and sew one to each side of the middle piece. If you have to use three lengths of 40″- 42″ wide fabric, then you should remove the selvedges from all the pieces and sew the three together length-wise (sometimes it works best to trim the middle piece to a smaller size first and then add strips to each side so that your seam are not too close to the outside edge of the backing. Press backing seams open.

Batting

Standard approximate pre-cut batting sizes are listed below (sizes are different with each company):

- Crib: 45″ x 60″
- Twin: 72″ x 90″
- Double: 80″ x 96″
- Queen: 90″ x 108″
- King: 120″ x 120″

When choosing a batting, you need to think about whether you are hand or machine quilting, how ose the stitches will be and how you want the quilt to look when finished, as well as how the quilt will be used when finished.

Batting can be made of many different types of fibers. If you like an old-fashioned looking quilt, you will probably want to use an all-cotton batting. Most newer cotton battings are bonded and do not require quilting stitches to be really close together the way that old battings once did. If you don't want to do a lot of quilting, use a regular or low-loft polyester batting.

If you are not sure which batting is right for your project, consult the professionals at your local quilt shop, where you can see samples of the different types of batting and quilts with different batting in them.

Layering the Quilt Sandwich
- A. First make sure your backing and top have been well-pressed and that your batting has been laid out to flatten as much as possible.
- B. Mark the middle of the backing and the quilt top on the wrong side on all four sides.
- C. Place backing right-side down on a smooth, flat surface (like the floor or several large tables put together). Using your hands, try to smooth the backing as flat as possible and pin or tape (using masking tape) the backing to your surface.
- D. Lay the batting over the backing, carefully smoothing it flat.

Layering the Quilt Sandwich *(cont.)*

E. Position quilt top on top of the batting carefully, making sure to avoid wrinkles in all three layers.

F. Match the centers of the sides of the quilt top with the centers of the backing.

G. Baste the backing, batting and top together using thread, curved safety pins or temporary basting spray adhesive to keep layers from shifting while quilting (read the next section for more basting details).

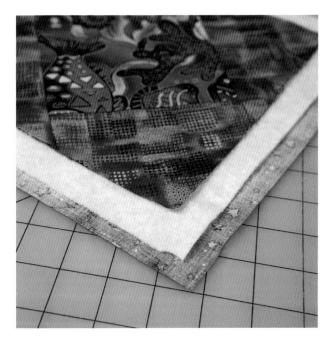

Layer your backing, batting and quilt top, being sure to leave 2″ - 4″ of backing and batting around each side.

Basting

Basting holds the backing, batting and the top of a quilt together to prevent shifting while quilting. Different types of basting are used depending on the type of quilting that will be done.

A. **Thread-basting using a long needle threaded with a long length of sewing thread:** Insert needle through all layers in center of quilt and baste layers together with a long (about 1″ - 2″ long) running stitch. For the first line of basting, stitch up and down the vertical center of the quilt. Next, baste across the horizontal center of the quilt. Working toward the edges and creating a grid, continue basting to completely stabilize the layers. This method is usually used for hand-quilting.

B. **Pin-basting using curved safety pins:** Begin in the center of the quilt and work outward to the edges, placing safety pins approximately every 4″. This method is better suited to machine-quilting.

C. **Spray-basting using temporary basting spray adhesive:** Carefully lift one corner of the batting from the backing and spray the basting spray. Carefully spread the batting back down starting in the middle of the top and spreading outwards towards the edges. Repeat this for the other three corners and then again repeat between the batting and the top of the quilt at all four corners in the same method. This is also a suitable method for machine-quilting.

D. When having a quilt quilted by a long-arm quilter, it is not necessary to baste in any way.

Quilting Instructions

Hand Quilting

Hand quilting features evenly spaced, small stitches on both sides of the quilt with no knots showing. Traditional quilters usually use 100% cotton thread in ecru or white, while more contemporary quilters tend to choose colors that coordinate with their quilt.

Beginners start with a size 8 or 9 "between" needle and advance to a shorter, finer size 10 or 12 needle for finer stitching. Use a well-fitting, puncture proof thimble on the middle finger of your sewing hand to position and push the needle through the quilt layers.

A frame or hoop keeps the layered quilt smooth and taunt; choose from a variety of shapes and sizes. Select a comfortable seat with proper back support and a good light source, preferably natural light, to reduce eye strain.

To begin, cut thread 24″ long and make a knot on one end. Place the needle tip either into a seam-line or 1″ behind the point where quilting stitches are to begin and guide it through the batting and up through the quilt top to "bury" the knot. Gently pull on the thread until you hear the knot "pop" through the quilt top. Trim the thread tail.

To quilt using a running stitch, hold the needle parallel to the quilt top and stitch up and down through the three layers with a rocking motion, making several stitches at a time. This technique is called "stacking". Gently and smoothly pull the thread through the layers. To end, make a small knot and bury it in the batting.

Machine Quilting

For machine quilting you need an even-feed or walking-foot to make sure you can quilt a straight stitch without shifting the layers and a darning or free-motion foot for free motion or really curvy stitching. It is sometimes helpful to use gloves with grips on the finger-tips to help hold the fabric as you move it around under the needle.

Use 100% cotton thread for machine quilting unless you want the stitches to be somewhat invisible, in which case you would use invisible monofilament thread (clear for light colored fabrics, smoky for dark fabric). Pre-test stitch length and thread tension using two muslin pieces layered with batting. Adjust as needed. If your machine's tension does not seem to like free-motion quilting you might try loosening the thread from the clip in the bobbin and you might find it works better (some think it is better to do this than to change the tension of your bobbin in any way).

Plan out how you are going to quilt your project first. You may want to stitch along the piecing lines of the quilt, which is called "stitching in the ditch". You can also trace designs onto the quilt top using an erasable drawing utensil or you can just free-form draw with the needle of the machine. Begin stitching in the middle of your project and work outward, making sure the layers are pulled tight. Roll the edges of the quilt toward the middle to allow you to get the project through your machine and carefully turn through the machine as you have to turn the project. There are several ways to start off machine quilting. You can start by putting the stitch length on zero and take a few stitches to knot the thread, you can just backstitch once or twice, or you can pull the bottom thread to the front of the quilt and tie it off and then use a needle to pull the thread tails into the quilt right where the knot is, so that you can pull the knot into the quilt. Trim any threads off if you leave any loose.

Binding Instructions

Bias binding is an outer finishing edge put on a quilt to cover the raw edges and give the quilt a nice finished look. Binding can be made with a fabric that matches the border or a complementary fabric.

There are many different ways to cut, sew and put on binding. The fabric is usually cut in 2 $^1/_4''$ strips, but can be anything from 2"- 3 $^1/_2''$ depending on how much you want to have visible. Make sure that whatever size you make the binding, you need to have it filled with the edge of the quilt. There should be no loose binding when you press the edge of the finished quilt between your fingers. Fabric for binding can be cut on the straight-grain or on the diagonal or bias grain. Many people use only one of the above mentioned ways to cut their binding. The best thing to do is to try both ways of doing it and pick the one you are most comfortable with and then practice it so that you get really good at it. I personally think that bias binding is the best binding to work with and is just as easy to make as straight-grain once you get over your initial fear of making it.

Cutting

Start with a square of fabric. Fold the square in half on the diagonal and press a crease into it. Open the square back up and cut your strips parallel to this original fold in the fabric. Cut your binding strips 2 $^1/_4''$ wide. There is another method for cutting bias if you have a cutting mat with the 45° angle marked on it. You can line up the fabric so that your straight edges are aligned with the straight horizontal and vertical lines on the mat and the 45° angle mark is visible above and below where your fabric lays. Use a 24" long ruler lined up along the 45° angle mark on the cutting mat to make your first cut. Then you can cut all your strips parallel to the first cut. When your fabric gets too long for the ruler, fold the fabric so that the cut edge is lined up on itself. As you get better at this you will be able to use a rectangle of fabric instead of a square if you choose, which will allow for longer strips.

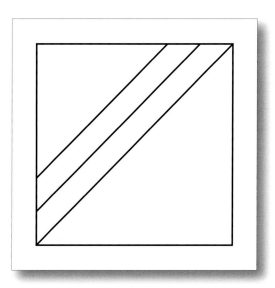

Connecting Pieces

Connect them to make a longer strip if needed by crossing two pieces of cut binding in a perpendicular manner and then making a seam at a 45° angle as seen in the diagram below. Make one long continuous strip of all your cut strips.

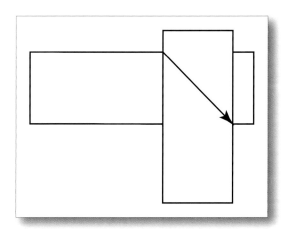

Lay the fabric strips of the cut binding right-sides together and sew a diagonal seam in a 45° angle.

Binding Instructions

Binding Edges

Fold the binding wrong sides together in half (lengthwise) and press. The binding is now 1 $\frac{1}{4}$″ wide. When you stitch the $\frac{1}{4}$″ seam allowance you will have 1″ left to pull around and stitch to the other side. You want the batting to completely fill the binding because it looks and it wears better. If you choose to use a wider binding then you will need to use a bigger seam allowance to make sure that the binding fits snuggly around the edge of your project.

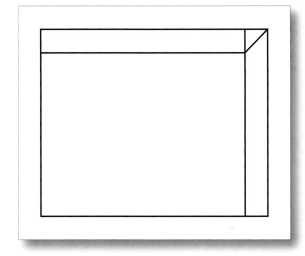

Fold the binding up to the top edge of the quilt and then back down, making sure that it has a 45° angle fold between the binding below and the strip that is loose. Lay the loose strip down along the quilt. Begin stitching $\frac{1}{4}$″ from the top edge of the quilt down the length of the quilt to the next corner.

The binding is generally machine stitched to the front or top side of a project and then hand-sewn to the bottom or back side of the project. Pin the binding to the top of the quilt down at the bottom edge by lining up the raw edges of the binding with the raw edge of the quilt making sure to leave a tail of about 12″ of binding hanging. Begin stitching the binding

with a $\frac{1}{4}$″ seam allowance. When you get near a corner stop $\frac{1}{4}$″ from the corner and then veer off the end in a 45° so that you sew right off the very point of he corner. Next, fold the binding up to the top edge of the quilt and then back down, making sure that it has a 45° angle fold between the binding below and the strip that is loose. Lay the loose strip down along the quilt. Begin stitching $\frac{1}{4}$″ from the top edge of the quilt down the length of the quilt to the next corner.

Mark a line at a 45 degree angle, then sew along the line to make your binding strips.

Open up the binding strip to make sure it is even before trimming the excess.

KITCHEN AND BEYOND

*Y*ou can make some great looking and very useful items for your kitchen using your stray quilt blocks. Make organization and storage fun by sewing these quick projects and putting them to good use. Chores, like cooking and setting the table can also be more fun with a cute apron, a pitcher cover and colorful placemats to liven up things.

Full Utility Apron

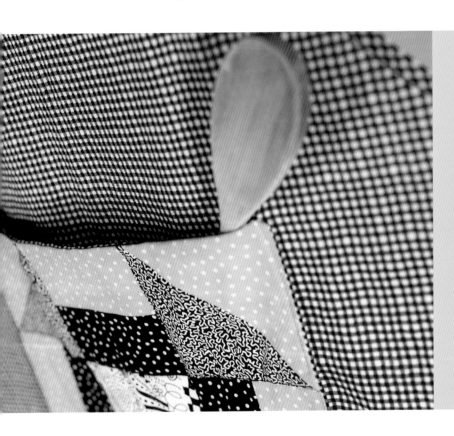

This is a really fun hostess gift to whip up or just make for yourself. It's easy to match it to a kitchen color theme, dishes and the other projects in this book.

21

Full Utility Apron

MATERIALS:

- One 12 ½" (12" finished) quilt block
- 1 yard fabric for apron
- 4 yards of bias binding or ribbon for the straps and finishing of the sides of the apron

INSTRUCTIONS:

Block

A. Layer the pieces for the block with the batting first, the backing face-up next and the pieced block face down last. Begin stitching in the middle of one side; sew around the outer edge of your block leaving a 5" opening on the side you started on. Trim the edges and corners neatly. Turn your block right-side out and poke out the corners. Fold in the fabric and batting at the opening and iron to prepare for sewing shut. Set aside for the next step.

Apron

B. Cut a 22" x 28" piece from the yard of fabric.
C. Fold the piece of fabric in half lengthwise so that it measures 11" x 28". Begin about ²/₃ of the way up from the bottom of the apron, on the outside edge, and shape the top of the apron by cutting away the material in a slight curve that runs from the side of the apron to the top of the apron.

Hem and finish bottom, and top edges of apron

D. Fold the bottom and top of the apron up 1" twice to cover the raw edge and topstitch using a complementary thread color right at the edges of the apron and the other edge of the fold to make the fold lay flat.
E. Finish the sides of the apron from the waist down by folding 1" twice so raw edge is folder under and topstitch with complementary thread.

Use binding or ribbon to make the ties and finish the upper curved edges of the apron.

F. Cut a piece of binding or ribbon long enough to make both a neck strap and a set of ties, one for each side of the apron. If you are using binding then fold the raw edges of the binding into the center so that they are not visible when the binding is folded.

G. Pin the binding or ribbon so that it folds over and covers the upper curved edges of the apron. Make sure to leave about 18" of binding at the top of the apron for a neck strap and about 18" of binding or ribbon on each side to use as ties for tying the apron around one's waist.
H. Topstitch along the inner edge of the ribbon or binding to finish it off.

Attach pieced quilt block

I. Pin the block into the lower middle of the apron and topstitch down one side, across the bottom and up the other side, leaving the top open to be a pocket.

CHURN DASH BLOCK

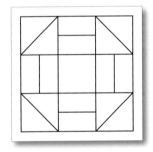

12" FINISHED BLOCK

(A) Two yellow 4 ⁷/₈" squares cut in half on the diagonal
(B) Two black and white checked 4 ⁷/₈" squares cut in half on the diagonal
(C) Two yellow 4 ½" x 2 ½" rectangles
(D) Two black with white print 4 ½" x 2 ½" rectangles
(E) One white with black print 4 ½" square

BLOCK PIECING INSTRUCTIONS:

A. Sew the pairs of triangles and the pairs of rectangles together as seen in the diagram above. Press the seams here towards the darker fabric.
B. Piece the sewn blocks into three rows and then the rows into a nine-patch to get the finished block.
C. When piecing the blocks into their rows, press the top and bottom rows' seams towards the center and the middle rows' seams towards the outside.
D. When piecing the rows together, press the row seams towards the center row.

Fun and Easy Pot Holder

$\mathcal{W}$e all need pot-holders for handling those hot dishes. When they're put to good use, pot-holders tend not to last very long so it's very helpful to be able to throw together new ones in a snap. They make great gifts as well.

Fun and Easy Potholder

MATERIALS:

- One 10 $\frac{1}{2}$″ - 12 $\frac{1}{2}$″ ($\frac{1}{2}$″ smaller finished) quilt block
- One piece of heat resistant batting the same size as the block
- Two pieces of cotton batting the same size as the block
- One piece of backing fabric the same size as the block

INSTRUCTIONS

A. Make a sandwich with the backing, the heat resistant batting, the two pieces of cotton batting and then the quilt block.

B. Quilt in the ditch around the pieces of the block or quilt in any other manner you choose.

C. Sew a binding around the block making a loop with the binding about 2″ long at one corner of the pot-holder.

DIAMOND IN A SQUARE BLOCK

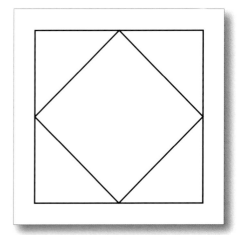

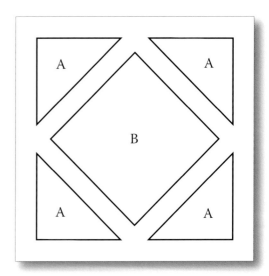

8″ FINISHED BLOCK

(A) Two 5 $\frac{3}{8}$″ yellow print squares cut in half once on the diagonal

(B) One 6 $\frac{7}{8}$″ blue fish print square

BLOCK PIECING INSTRUCTIONS:

A. Sew a yellow triangle to two opposing sides of the fish square and then sew triangles to the other two sides, pressing the seams out towards the corners.

Fun and Easy Potholder

Decorative Toaster Cover

 oes your toaster have a permanent place on your kitchen counter? Do you wish you could make it disappear, especially when you have company? This is the perfect chance to add some of your favorite art form to your kitchen with a cute toaster-cover.

Decorative Toaster Cover

MATERIALS:

- **One or two 6 ¹/₂" (6" finished) pieced quilt blocks**
- **One or two 6 ¹/₂" blocks of coordinating fabric to use for backing pieced blocks**
- **One or two 6 ¹/₂" pieces of thin cotton batting**
  Note: An alternative is piece the blocks into the fabric that you use for the outside of your cover. With this method you would not need backing and batting for the 6" blocks.
- **1 yard of main background fabric for the outside of the cover**
- **1 yard lining fabric for the underside of the cover**
- **1 yard thin cotton batting**
- **¹/₂ yard piece of fabric to use for binding**

INSTRUCTIONS:

Make three important measurements

A. First, measure your toaster. Measure the width across the top and bottom of the toaster (the measurements should be about 12" - 16" depending on the type of toaster. This is a general range of sizes for most of the common toasters. If you are working with a special toaster, an antique one of some kind, use those dimensions and follow the instructions).

B. Second, measure the height of the toaster (this should be about 7" - 10"). Measure the depth of the toaster from front to back (this measurement should be about 6" - 9").

C. Finally, measure from the bottom of one side of your toaster over the top and down the other side in an upside-down U shape (this measurement should be about 24" - 32").

Note: If you choose to piece your blocks into the cover then you should first subtract the size of your quilt block from the overall measurement you need for the sides of your toaster. Divide the remaining width and height by two to get the size of strips you need to add to the blocks to piece your side panels. You will need to add about ¹/₂" to each strip to allow for seam allowances. Then cut your batting and lining fabric accordingly.

Make pieced quilt blocks for decorating the cover.

D. Layer together the 6" blocks, begin with the batting first, the backing face-up next and the pieced block face-down last.

E. Begin in the middle of one side, and sew around the outer edge of each block. Stop stitching about 2 ¹/₂" from where you began to leave an opening through which the block is turned right side out.

F. Turn your blocks right-side out and poke out the corners so they are sharp and crisp.

G. At the opening iron the seam allowances toward the inside in preparation for sewing the opening closed. Set these aside for the next step.

Cut pieces for the cover.

H. Cut out the three pieces of the main background fabric for the outside, the pieces of lining and the pieces of batting. The size will be determined by the three measurements you made.
    Note: if you plan to use quilt blocks as pockets stitched to the outside of the cover, you can simplify at this step by layering the whole piece of main background fabric, the lining fabric and the batting. If you are piecing the blocks into the cover fabric then you will need to follow the note mentioned above for measuring and then sew the blocks and border strips into the pieces that you will use for your cover pieces.

I. Layer each set of lining pieces and outer pieces of fabric with batting and quilt in any manner you choose.

Attach blocks to each of the two side panels.

J. Pin a quilted block to each of the two side panels, or the front and back panel, for the cover, making sure that the hole is pinned and facing down.

K. Top-stitch the quilt blocks to their cover pieces, making sure that the seam allowance of the opening in the blocks is caught in the top-stitching.

Decorative Toaster Cover

Bind and assemble the pieces into a cover.

L. Make or buy 3 yards of bias binding. Cut the binding into three 1 yard pieces. You will use one for each of the two sides of the cover and one for the bottom edge of the cover (see general instructions for making bias binding).

M. Pin the binding and front panel of your cover to the long top panel, lining up raw edges and matching the front panel and top panel at one corner to start your sewing. Stitch together with the seam on the outside of the cover. Follow the same instructions with the back panel, starting at the same end as the front.

N. Trim off any extra fabric on the top panel at the end.

O. Fold the binding over the seams and hand-sew on with a blind-hem stitch.

P. Machine-sew the binding on the outside bottom edge of the cover and fold over to hand-sew the binding on the inside of the cover.

Suggestions for quilting:

A nice machine quilting pattern for these covers is to quilt about 2″ apart in diagonal lines that cross each other so that you have a diamond pattern. This also works well with spray basting to make it even easier.

Depending on the fabric one chooses for the cover, a nice effect can be achieved if you hand quilt and use a pattern that accentuates the pattern in your fabric, or outlines key images in the fabric.

SQUARE WITH BORDERS IN A DIAMOND BLOCK

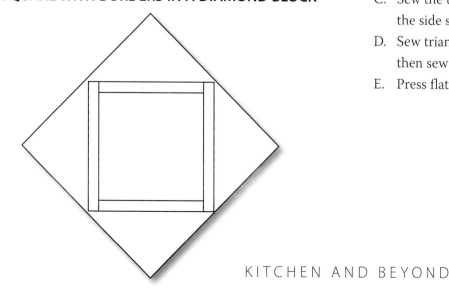

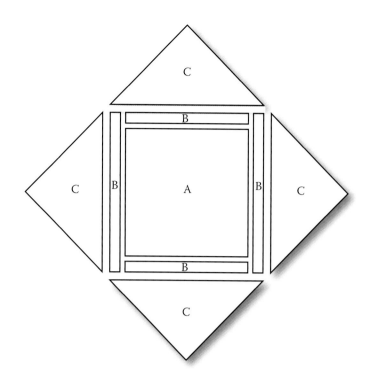

4″ X 5″ FINISHED BLOCK

This is a good block to make to high-light a specific part of a focus fabric.

(A) One 3 $^{1}/_{2}$″ x 4 $^{1}/_{2}$″ piece of a focus fabric

(B) Four 1 $^{1}/_{2}$″ x 10 ″ blue strips

(C) Two 4″ red squares cut in half once on the diagonal

BLOCK PIECING INSTRUCTIONS:

A. Cut out the focus fabric into a 3 $^{1}/_{2}$″ x 4 $^{1}/_{2}$″ rectangle.

B. Cut two 1 $^{1}/_{2}$″ x 3 $^{1}/_{2}$″ strips and two 1 $^{1}/_{2}$″ x 6″ of blue fabric for borders.

C. Sew the top and bottom strips on first and then the side strips.

D. Sew triangles onto two opposite sides of block and then sew the remaining two triangles on.

E. Press flat and trim to square.

Log Cabin Placemats

$\mathcal{T}$hese bright placemats will make meal time seem like a party. Your guests will feel like you really fussed over them--especially kids! Be prepared to make more when your friends get a look at these.

Log Cabin Placemats

MATERIALS:

- **Four 12 1/2″ (12″ finished) Log Cabin quilt blocks**
- **1/2 yard of coordinating fabric to border the blocks or four different fat quarters**
- **1 yard of coordinating fabric for backing of placemats**
- **1 1/4 yards of coordinating fabric for binding or 9 yards of ready-made binding**
- **1 yard of thin cotton batting (you can use a heat resistant batting if you choose)**

INSTRUCTIONS:

A. First, border each Log Cabin block with 1 1/2″ x 12 1/2″ strips on the top and bottom and 3 1/2″ x 15″ strips on the sides. The placemat should measure about 15″ x 20″ when you are done. Trim all to the same size.

B. Cut four pieces of backing fabric 16″ x 21″. Cut four pieces of batting the same size. Layer each placemat for quilting and quilt in any manner you choose (these placemats were long-arm quilted).

C. Make 9 yards of bias binding, use leftovers from a previous project or buy ready-made bias binding. Cut the binding into four equal pieces so you will have a piece for each placemat (see general instructions for making bias binding).

D. Sew binding onto the front side of each placemat. Fold binding over to the back and hand sew.

12″ FINISHED BLOCK

Note: One fat quarter each rectangle of 6 different brights to piece the blocks out of.

(A) One 2 1/2″ x 3 1/2″ rectangle
(B) One 3″ x 3 1/2″ rectangle
(C) Two 2″ x 5″ rectangles
(D) Two 2″ x 6 1/2″ rectangles
(E) Two 2″ x 8″ rectangles
(F) Two 2″ x 9 1/2″ rectangles
(G) Two 2″ x 11″ rectangles
(H) One 2″ x 12 1/2″ rectangle

BLOCK PIECING INSTRUCTIONS:

A. Start with the small square and add the smallest rectangle to one side.

B. Going in a counter-clockwise direction, sew each set of next sized larger strips to the block as seen in the diagram opposite.

LOG CABIN BLOCK

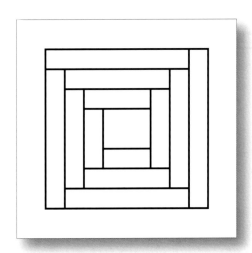

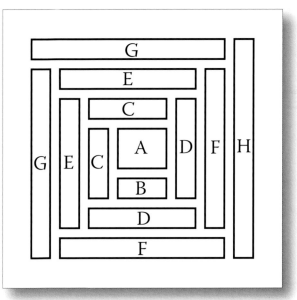

Picnic Placemats

*J*oin the ants for a great outdoor meal using these cute placemats. They'll liven up any picnic. You'll love the handy little pockets for the silverware.

MATERIALS:

- **Four 12 $^1/_2$″ (12″ finished) Churn Dash quilt blocks**
- **$^1/_2$ yard of fabric to border the blocks**
- **1 yard of fabric for backing of placemats (the same fabric was used for the background of the blocks, the borders, the utensil holders, and the backings in this project)**
- **Four 8″ squares of coordinating fabric for utensil holders**
- **1$^1/_4$ yard of fabric for binding or 10 yards of ready-made binding (black fabric was used for this project)**
- **1 yard of thin cotton batting (you can use a heat resistant batting if you choose)**

INSTRUCTIONS:

A. First border each churn dash block with 1 $^1/_2$″ x 12 $^1/_2$″ strips on the top and bottom, a 2 $^1/_2$″ x 15″ strip on the left side of the block and a 5 $^1/_2$″ x 15″ strip on the right side. The placemat should measure about 15″ x 20″ when you are done. Trim all to the same size.

B. Cut four pieces of backing fabric 16″ x 21″. Cut four pieces of batting the same size. Layer each placemat for quilting and quilt in any manner you choose (these placemats were long-arm quilted which would require your backing to be larger than the top by about 5″).

C. Fold the 8″ squares in half, right-sides together, and stitch up the two sides of each folded piece. Leave the end opposite the fold open. Turn right side out and iron well.

D. Pin one of these pieces to each placemat at the bottom right corner of the placemat, making sure the edges are lined up on the bottom and right side of the two pieces. The open side of the utensil holder should be lined up with raw edges of the right side of each placemat. Topstitch the left side of the utensil holder into place on the placemat (the right side and bottom will get sewn on with the binding).

E. Make 9 yards of bias binding. Use leftovers from a previous project or buy ready-made bias binding. Cut the binding into four equal pieces so you will have a piece for each placemat (see general instructions for making bias binding).

F. Sew binding onto the right side of the placemat making sure the utensil holder is sewn into the binding seam. Fold binding over to the back and hand sew.

CHURN DASH BLOCK

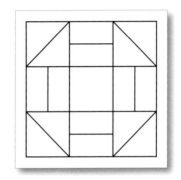 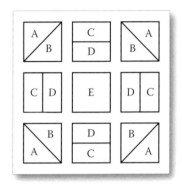

12″ FINISHED BLOCK

(A) Two 4 $^7/_8$″ red check squares cut in half on the diagonal

(B) Two 4 $^7/_8$″ black squares cut in half on the diagonal

(C) Two 4 $^1/_2$″ x 2 $^1/_2$″ red check rectangles

(D) Two 4 $^1/_2$″ x 2 $^1/_2$″ black rectangles

(E) One 4 $^1/_2$″ red check square

BLOCK PIECING INSTRUCTIONS:

E. Sew the pairs of triangles and the pairs of rectangles together as seen in the diagram above. Press the seams here towards the darker fabric.

F. Piece the sewn blocks into three rows and then the rows into a nine-patch to get the finished block.

G. When piecing the blocks into their rows, press the top and bottom row's seams towards the center and the middle row's seams towards the outside.

H. When piecing the rows together, press the row seams towards the center row.

Lunch Bag

$\mathcal{D}$o you take a lunch to work each day? Well this is the perfect little bag to pack up some midday sustenance with a little flair. It could also be used as a project bag, a gift bag for a special gift, or for anything else that calls for a small bag.

Lunch Bag

MATERIALS:
- One canvas lunch sack
- One 4 $\frac{1}{2}$″ (4″ finished) quilt block
- Four 1″ strips of a coordinating fabric
- One 4 $\frac{1}{2}$″ piece of batting

INSTRUCTIONS:
A. Border the quilt block by sewing a strip to each side of the block and then one to the top and bottom of the block.
B. Center the batting on the back of the block and quilt in the ditch on the block.
C. Fold the strips around to the back like binding and baste in place to the batting.
D. Topstitch the block in place in the center of the bag or hand-sew with a blind-hem stitch and you are finished.

ECONOMY PATCH BLOCK

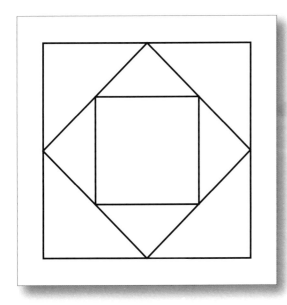

4″ FINISHED BLOCK
(A) Two 2 $\frac{7}{8}$″ light blue marble squares cut in half once on the diagonal
(B) One 3 $\frac{3}{4}$″ dark blue print square cut twice on the diagonal
(C) One 2 $\frac{1}{2}$″ light blue dot print square

BLOCK PIECING INSTRUCTIONS:
A. Sew the four dark blue triangles to the center square.
B. Sew the light blue triangles to the new pieced center square.

Tea Cover

o you have big meals where you set out big pitchers of drink and bowls of food? Flies love the food and drink as much as your guests do. This project is the perfect way to keep those pesky insects out of your food while also dressing up your outdoor table. This is another great gift item.

Tea Cover

MATERIALS:

- One 12 $\frac{1}{2}''$ - 14 $\frac{1}{2}''$ ($\frac{1}{2}''$ smaller finished) quilt block for each food cover
- One piece of backing the same size as each quilt block
- One piece of very thin batting or interfacing the same size as each block
- 1$\frac{1}{2}$ yards of binding for each cover
- Four marble-sized beads for the corners of each cover

INSTRUCTIONS:

A. Layer each backing, batting and block together to be quilted and quilt in a way you choose.
B. Machine-sew the binding onto the front of each quilted block and turn over to the back to hand-sew.
C. Sew a bead to each corner of the cover.

Note: The beads add weight to the cover to help hold it in place over your food bowl or pitcher.

TEA COVER BLOCK

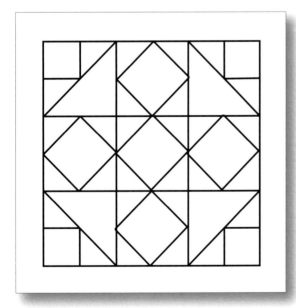

12″ FINISHED BLOCK

(A) Four 2 $\frac{1}{2}''$ blue squares

(B) Twelve 2 $\frac{7}{8}''$ white squares cut on the diagonal

(C) Two 2 $\frac{7}{8}''$ pink dot squares cut on the diagonal

(D) Two 4 $\frac{7}{8}''$ pink dot squares cut on the diagonal

(E) Four multi batik squares

(F) One 3 $\frac{3}{8}''$ purple square

BLOCK PIECING INSTRUCTIONS:

A. Sew four sets of the two small triangles and one small square into the larger triangles seen at the outer corners of the block, pressing the seams toward the square. Sew the pieced triangles to the cut triangles to make blocks, pressing the seams toward the larger triangle.
B. Sew five sets of four small triangles and one 3 $\frac{3}{8}''$ square into the blocks seen in the center of the larger block, pressing the seams toward the triangles.
C. Sew all the smaller pieced blocks into a nine-patch, pressing the seams of the top and bottom rows one way and the middle row the opposite way.

Tea Cover

The beaded corners add charm to this wonderfully simple piece.

Decorative Half Apron and Hotpad

$\mathcal{T}$his frilly and stylish apron is just the ticket when you want to look great while you are whipping up dinner. It can even be worn over an under-skirt as an accessory for an outfit.

Decorative Half Apron and Hotpad

MATERIALS:

- $^3/_4$ yard piece of fabric for apron
- A strip of fabric for waist-band that is 4 $^1/_2$″ wide and equal to your waist measurement plus 25″ for the length.
- One 8 $^1/_2$″ (8″ finished) quilt block of your choice (a saw tooth star is used in this project)
- One 8 $^1/_2$″ piece of coordinating fabric for the backing of the block
- Optional $^1/_4$ yard of contrasting fabric for pleated ruffle

INSTRUCTIONS:

Block

A. Put together the 8 $^1/_2$″ block with the batting first, the backing face-up next, and the pieced block face-down last. Begin stitching in the middle of one side; sew around the outer edge of your block leaving a 4″ opening on the side where you started. Trim the edges and corners neatly. Turn your block right-side out and poke out the corners. Fold in the fabric and batting at the opening and iron in preparation for sewing shut. Set aside for the next step.

Apron

B. First cut a piece of fabric 26 $^1/_2$″ wide x 17 $^1/_2$″ long for the apron body.
C. Make the pleats at the waistband of the apron by placing pins 3 $^1/_2$″, 6″ and 8 $^1/_2$″ in from each side of the main apron piece. Fold in the two outer pins at each side (the ones at the 3 $^1/_2$″ and 8 $^1/_2$″ spots) into the middle pin (the one at the 6″ spot) to make the pleats and pin in place.
D. Fold the waist-band piece of fabric in half down the length and press the fold in. Set aside for later.
E. Cut the selvage off the $^1/_4$ yard piece of fabric and cut it into four 2″ strips. Sew the four strips together to make a 106″ long, 2″ wide strip. Fold in half lengthwise. To pleat, take $^1/_2$″ folds in the folded 2″ strips towards each other in a similar manner to the pleat in the waist of the apron above, but on a smaller scale.
F. Pin the pleated ruffle, right sides together to the sides and bottom of the apron.
G. Sew the pleated ruffle to the apron down one side across the bottom and up the other side. Pull back and press flat.
H. Fold the strip for the waist-band right-sides together. Lay the apron on the waist, centering it. Put pins in the waist-band at apron edges. Set the apron aside.
I. Sew a $^1/_2$″ seam along the raw edges of the waist-band from the outer ends to the pins. There should be a space for turning left the same size as the top measurement of the apron. Turn the waist-band right-side out and press in the seam allowance of the opening.
J. Place the top of the apron into the opening of the waist-band so the waistband covers the top of the apron on the front and the back and the top of the apron touches the inside of the fold of the waist-band. Top-stitch the opening of the waist-band closed right along the very edge, making sure to catch the apron inside.

OHIO STAR BLOCK

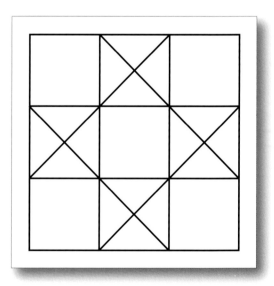

8″ FINISHED BLOCK

(A) Four 3 ¹/₈″ pink squares

(B) Two 3 ⁷/₈″ bluesquare cut in half twice on the diagonal

(C) Two 3 ⁷/₈″ pink squares cut in half twice on the diagonal

(D) One 3 ¹/₈ blue print square

BLOCK PIECING INSTRUCTIONS:

This block is constructed as a nine-patch that has two narrow rows and one wider row in the center.

A. First sew eight pink triangles and eight blue triangles into quarter square triangle units. You can use any method of triangle piecing to get your four quarter square units.

B. Sew two rows of the pink squares and one quarter square unit together and press seams toward the outside.

C. Sew the middlerow with two quarter square units and one blue square in the center.

D. Sew the rows togetheras shown in the diagram opposite.

E. Sew these two rows to the center row as seen in the diagram of block. When piecing the triangles together, press the seams out towards the smaller triangles.

F. On the top and bottom row press the seams from the center out towards each side.

G. On the middle row press the seams from the out side in towards the center of the block.

Fun Easy Pot Holder

We all need pot-holders in our kitchens for handling hot dishes. Pot-holders tend not to last very long when they are put to good use so it is very helpful to be able to throw together new ones in a snap. They make great gifts, as well.

This is an especially good project to make in matching fabric as either of the aprons in this book and even the toaster cover.

MATERIALS:

A. One 10 ¹/₂″ - 12 ¹/₂″ (¹/₂″ smaller finished) quilt block

B. One piece of heat resistant batting the same size as the block

C. Two pieces of cotton batting the same size as the block

D. One piece of backing fabric the same size as the block

INSTRUCTIONS:

1. Make a sandwich with the backing, the heat resistant batting, the two pieces of cotton batting and then the quilt block.

2. Quilt in the ditch around the pieces of the block or quilt in any other manner you choose.

3. Sew a binding around the block making a loop with the binding about 2″ long at one corner of the pot-holder

AROUND THE HOUSE

$\mathcal{Q}$uilted projects are a great way to decorate the rooms in your house. There are many ways to use your quilting for decorating other than just by making quilts. This chapter has several easy home-decorating projects that incorporate your quilting passion to your home décor.

Sleepy Sailing Quilt

$\mathcal{D}$o you wish sometimes you had more time in your life to make quilts as gifts? This is a great quilt for a child. It takes only a few pieced blocks, 12 $^1/_2$″ squares of a coordinating fabric and one large border. You can use it together with the Wall-hanging Headboard, the Tab Curtains, and the director's chair for a cute bedroom decorating theme.

Sleepy Sailing Quilt

MATERIALS:

- **Five 12 ½" (12" finished) pieced blocks**
- **Ten 12 ½" squares of coordinating fabric** (turquoise water fabric was used for this project)
- **3 ½ yards of coordinating fabric for borders** (blue sky fabric was used for this project)
- **5 yards of fabric for a backing (or 2 yards of 108" wide fabric)**
- **One twin size batting**

INSTRUCTIONS:

A. Lay out the blocks and squares in a pattern that you like.

B. Sew the blocks and squares together in rows of three and then sew the rows together.

C. Measure the final size of the finished top and set aside for sewing on the borders.

Preparing and sewing on the borders

D. Cut the selvedge off the border fabric.

E. Cut eight 14 ½" strips of the border fabric.

F. Sew together four pairs of border strips so that you have four long pieces.

G. Cut two of the strips the same size as the side measurement of the quilt top and sew to the sides of the quilt top.

H. Measure across the top and the bottom of the quilt top.

I. Cut two strips for the top and the bottom of the quilt top the same size as top and bottom measurements and sew onto the top and bottom of the quilt top.

Preparing the backing

J. Cut your 5 yard piece of fabric into two 2 ½ yard pieces.

K. Cut off all of the selvedges.

L. Cut one piece in half down the length on the fold so you have two pieces that are about 21" x 2 ½ yards long.

M. Sew one of the 21" wide pieces to each side of the bigger piece.

Preparing for quilting

N. Layer the backing, batting and top together to be quilted.

O. Pin, spray, or thread-baste for hand or machine quilting. If you choose to have the quilt long-arm quilted, then do not baste at all and make sure your backing is at least 5" larger than your top all the way around.

Binding

P. Make or buy 9 ½ yards of bias binding

Q. Machine-sew the binding on the front side of the quilt and turn over to hand-sew onto the back side of the quilt.

FIFTY-FOUR-FORTY OR FLIGHT BLOCK

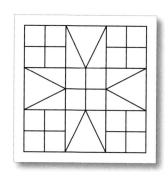

12" FINISHED BLOCK

(A) Four 2 ⅝" x 5 ¼" red & orange stripe rectangles in two pairs facing each other and cut them in half on the diagonal

(B) Four 4 ⅞" blue water print squares. Draw lines from one corner to the opposite side at the center and then back to the other corner as seen in the diagram

(C) Six 2 ½" orange squares

(D) Six 2 ½" yellow squares

(E) Eight 2 ½" blue water squares

BLOCK PIECING INSTRUCTIONS:

A. Press the top and bottom row seams going in one direction and the middle row going in the opposite direction. Press the top horizontal row seam up and the bottom one down.

Sleepy Sailing Quilt

SAILING SHIP BLOCK

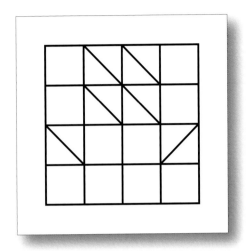

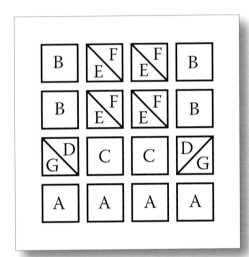

Note: You can alternate the direction of the sails as seen in Sleepy Sailing Quilt on pg. 48 and the Pocket Tab Curtain on pg. 54 by rotating the position of the half-square triangle blocks.

12″ FINISHED BLOCK

(A) **Four 3 ¹/₂″ green or blue squares for the water at the bottom**

(B) **Four 3 ¹/₂″ blue squares for the sky**

(C) **Two 3 ¹/₂″ red squares for the boat**

(D) **One 3 ⁷/₈″ red square cut on the diagonal**

(E) **Two 3 ⁷/₈″ yellow squares cut on the diagonal**

(F) **Two 3 ⁷/₈″ blue squares cut on the diagonal for the sky against the sails of the ship**

(G) **One 3 ⁷/₈″ green or blue square cut on the diagonal bottom sides of the boat**

BLOCK PIECING INSTRUCTIONS:

A. Sew your triangles into half-squares.

B. Sew your blocks into rows.

C. Sew the rows into the block.

Press each row's seam in the opposite direction from the row above or below it. The only exception is the center of the sail where you should carefully pull the stitches out of the seam allowance and press all the seams in one direction clockwise or counter-clockwise (whichever the fabric seems to want to go). This will make the block lay flatter.

DOUBLE SAW-TOOTH STAR BLOCK

Sleepy Sailing Quilt

12″ FINISHED BLOCK WITH A 6″ FINISHED BLOCK IN THE MIDDLE SQUARE

6″ finished block

(A) One 3 ½″ orange square ☐

(B) Four 2 ⅞″ red squares cut in half on the diagonal ◹

(C) One 4 ¼″ yellow square cut twice on the diagonal ⊠

(D) Four 2″ yellow squares ☐

12″ finished block

(E) One 6 ½″ square (this will be the 6″ block from the directions above) ☐

(F) Four 3 ⅞″ red squares cut in half on the diagonal ◹

(G) One 7 ¼″ blue water print square cut twice on the diagonal ⊠

(H) Four 4″ blue water print squares ☐

BLOCK PIECING INSTRUCTIONS:

Sew the smaller block together first and then use it as the center block for the larger block.

A. Next sew the four units that consist of a yellow triangle and two red triangles.

B. Sew two of the yellow triangle segments to the center block to form the center row of the smaller block.

C. Sew two yellow squares to the ends of two of the yellow triangle segments.

D. Sew these two rows to the center row as seen in the diagram of block.

E. Sew the pieces together as seen in the diagram for the 12″ block, substituting blue for the large triangles and the outer square corners and using the 6″ block as the center square.

F. When piecing the triangles together, press the seams out towards the smaller triangles.

G. On the top and bottom row of each block press the seams from the center out towards each side.

H. On the middle row of each block press the seams from the outside in towards the center of the block.

MICHAEL'S STAR BLOCK

12″ FINISHED BLOCK

- Four copies of the foundation pattern for the spires and of the outer edge of the block
- One copy of the foundation pattern of the circle

(A) Four 4 ½″ x 6 ½″ yellow rectangles ☐

(B) Eight 4 ½″ x 6 ½″ red & orange stripe rectangles ☐

(C) Sixteen 2 ½″ x 3 ½″ red rectangles ☐

(D) Thirty two 2 ½″ x 3″ blue water print rectangles ☐

(E) One 4″ square of yellow print to trace the center circle onto (the piece for this block was fussy-cut from celestial print fabric) ☐

(F) Four 4″ x 6″ rectangles pieced by sewing a 2″ x 6½″ strip of light yellow and a 2″ x 6½″ strip of dark yellow together ☐

(G) One fat quarter of the blue water print for the edge of pieced circle

Note: Make eight copies of Unit A. Cut four apart on the dotted lines. Piece smaller pieces of fabric into larger units in the order of their numbers plus letters.

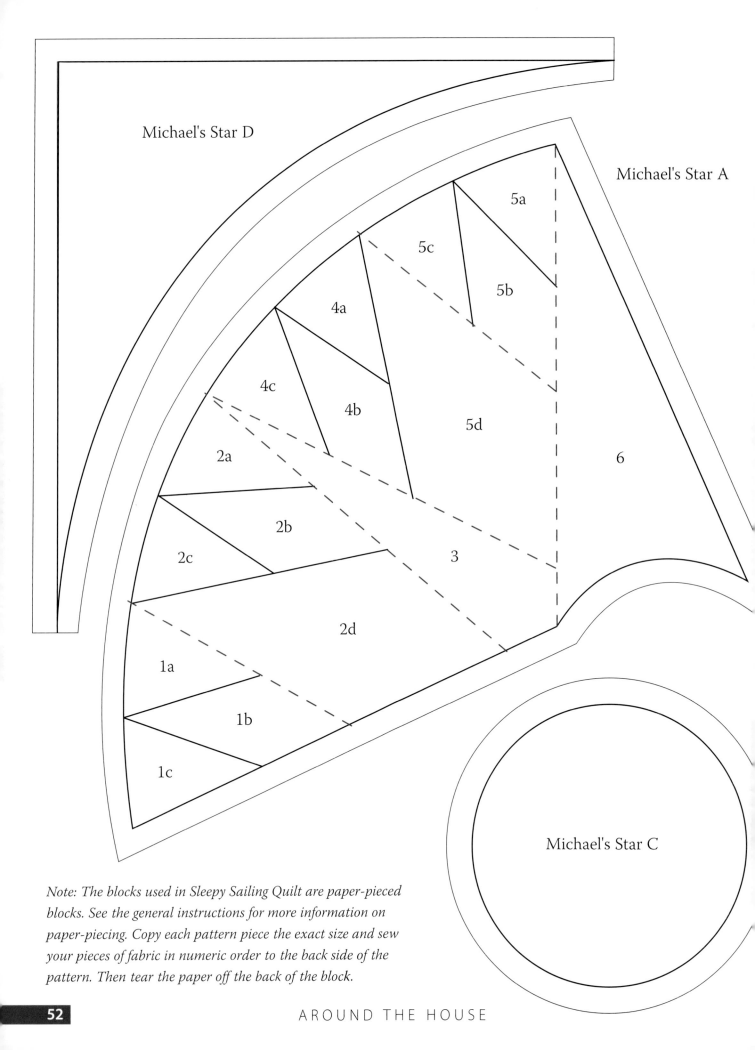

Michael's Star D

Michael's Star A

5a

5c

5b

4a

4c

4b

5d

6

2a

2b

2c

3

2d

1a

1b

1c

Michael's Star C

Note: The blocks used in Sleepy Sailing Quilt are paper-pieced blocks. See the general instructions for more information on paper-piecing. Copy each pattern piece the exact size and sew your pieces of fabric in numeric order to the back side of the pattern. Then tear the paper off the back of the block.

Pocket Tab Curtains

$\mathcal{T}$ ab curtains with quilt blocks topstitched to the curtain make a fun and simple way to organize and store toys, books and even sewing or craft supplies. These curtains use the quilt blocks shown in the Sleepy Sailing Quilt.

Pocket Tab Curtains

MATERIALS:

- **Three to eight 8 1/2″ - 10 1/2″ (1/2″ smaller finished) quilt blocks depending on how much curtain you have**
- **Batting or flannel squares the same size as the quilt blocks you choose**
- **One backing square the same size as the blocks you choose**
- **3/4 yards of coordinating fabric for binding (red fabric was used in this project)**
- **Fabric for curtains: the amount depends on the measurements of your windows**

INSTRUCTIONS FOR MEASURING FOR CURTAINS:

A. Measure width and length of your window. You can either measure the inside measurement of the window frame or the outside measurements of the frame depending on where you want to hang the curtain panel.

B. Next, double the width to allow for proper hanging and add 10″ to the length. Now you are ready to buy your fabric.

C. You will need 1/2 yard of the same fabric or a complementary fabric for the tabs at the top and the band at the hem.

D. Purchase machine thread in a complementary color for top-stitching

INSTRUCTIONS FOR MAKING CURTAINS:

E. Cut the fabric to the required measurements, adding an extra 1″ seam allowance for the sides and 6″ for the top and bottom.

F. Cut enough pairs of 3″ x 9″ strips to have tabs every 6″ across the top of your panel.

G. Sew a double-fold 1/2″ seam down each side of your panel using a complementary thread color.

H. Sew a double-fold 3″ hem on the bottom and top of the panel.

I. Cut strips of your binding the same size as the width of your curtain panels and fold the raw edges into the middle of the strip and press flat.

J. Pin a strip to each panel at the bottom hem

stitches. Top-stitch each edge of the strip (right at the folded edge) to the panel.

K. Next, iron a 1/2″ seam on both sides of each 3″ strip.

L. Sew the strips, right sides together using a top-stitch right along the edge of the strip and a complementary thread color.

M. Fold these strips in half and stitch to the top of your panel about 1″ from the top and right (see diagram below)

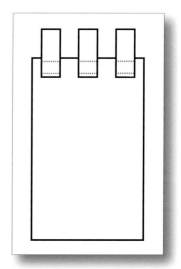

QUILT THE BLOCKS FOR POCKETS:

N. Layer each block with its backing and batting and quilt in any way you choose.

O. Sew a binding on each block.

FINISH BY TOPSTITCHING POCKETS TO CURTAINS:

P. Pin each block to the curtain panel in any layout you choose.

Q. Top stitch in the ditch along the inner edge of the binding on your quilt blocks down one side, across the bottom, and up the other side with a complementary color thread. Now you are ready to hang the curtains and have a fun, attractive way to organize and store toys, crafts, kitchen tools, office supplies.

Sailing Ship Diagram on page 50
Double Saw-Tooth Star Diagram on page 50

Wall Hanging Headboard

*T*his is an easy project that will liven up the head of a bed without having a headboard. It's such a simple way to make a room more homey. What child wouldn't love to have this starry night sky at the head of their bed?

Wall Hanging Headboard

MATERIALS:

- One 10 $\frac{1}{2}$" (10" finished) quilt block (a ship block is used here)
- One 14 $\frac{1}{2}$" square of interlining or thin batting
- One 14 $\frac{1}{2}$" square of backing fabric
- A small handful of stuffing
- Two pieces of fabric measuring 20" high x 40" wide (a blue star fabric is used in this project)
- One 20" x 40" piece of batting (high-loft batting is nice for this project, but is more difficult to quilt)
- $\frac{3}{4}$ yard piece of fabric for bias binding or 5 yards of ready-made bias binding for the quilt and block (red is used in this project)

INSTRUCTIONS:

A. Start with a 10 $\frac{1}{2}$" ship block and sew 2 $\frac{1}{2}$" strips around, mitering the corners if you choose. Trim the block to 14 $\frac{1}{2}$".

B. Layer the interlining and the ship block. Quilt in the ditch around the pieces of the block.

C. Cut small cross-cuts in the interlining behind each sail of the ship and stuff each sail with stuffing so the sails look like they have wind blowing in them.

D. Pin the backing fabric in place under the block and sew a binding around the block.

E. Layer the two 20" x 40" pieces of fabric with the batting in between and spray or pin baste for quilting. Hand or machine quilt in any manner you choose. The sample pictured here has been quilted with diagonal lines from both corners that form diamonds.

F. Make 4 $\frac{1}{2}$ yards of bias binding (see general instructions for making binding). Fold the binding around to the back side and hand-sew.

G. Pin the finished block to the middle of the background. Sew the block onto the background quilt, stitching in the ditch next to the block's binding, either all the way around or just the sides and bottom. Leave the top open to be a pocket.

Optional:

You can make a hanging sleeve for the back of this project. For a hanging sleeve you need a 40" x 8" strip of fabric. Sew a $\frac{1}{2}$" double-fold seam on the two sides of this piece so it becomes 38" x 8". Fold this piece in half lengthwise with the right-sides together and sew together with a $\frac{1}{2}$" seam. Turn right-side out, press flat with the seam in the middle of one side, and sew to the upper back of the quilt using a blind-hem stitch at the top and bottom of the fabric tube.

SAILING SHIP BLOCK

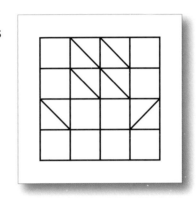

10" FINISHED BLOCK

(A) **Four 3" green or blue squares for the water at the bottom**

(B) **Four 3" blue squares for the sky**

(C) **Two 3" red squares for the boat**

(D) **One 3 $\frac{7}{8}$" red square cut on the diagonal**

(E) **Two 3 $\frac{7}{8}$" yellow squares cut on the diagonal**

(F) **Two 3 $\frac{7}{8}$" blue sky print squares cut on the diagonal for the sky against the sails of the ship**

(G) **One 3 $\frac{7}{8}$" green or blue water print square cut on the diagonal bottom sides of the boat**

BLOCK PIECING INSTRUCTIONS:

A. Sew your triangles into half-squares.

B. Sew your blocks into rows.

C. Sew the rows into the block.

Press each row's seam in the opposite direction from the row above or below it. The only exception is the center of the sail, where you should carefully pull the stitches out of the seam allowance and press all the seams in one direction clockwise or counter-clockwise (whichever the fabric seems to want to go). This will make the block lay flatter.

Snazzy Store-Bought Pillow

$\mathcal{I}$f you don't want to make a pillow with a quilt
block, then just buy a pillow and hand-sew a quilted
block to one or both sides. A bright solid colored pillow
works well for this project.

Snazzy Store Bought Pillow

MATERIALS:

- One or more 12″ - 20″ store-bought pillows of your choice (a 16″ pillow was used for this project)
- One or two 6 1/2″ -10 1/2″ (1/2″ smaller finished) quilt blocks per pillow (one 8 1/2″, 8″ finished, block was used for this project)
- One piece of batting for each block the same size as the block
- One fat quarter of a coordinating fabric for binding

INSTRUCTIONS:

A. Cut four 1″ strips for each block from the fat quarter (cut the strips a little longer than the length of the block).

B. Sew a strip to each side of the block and then one to the top and bottom of the block.

C. Center the batting on the back of the block and quilt in the ditch around the piecing in the block.

D. Fold the strips around to the back like binding and baste in place to the batting

E. Hand-stitch the block to the pillow using a blind-hem stitch, making sure to center the block on the face of the pillow.

SAILING SHIP BLOCK

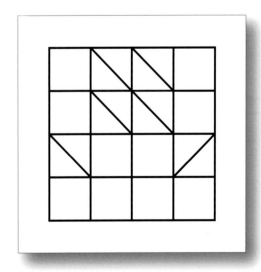

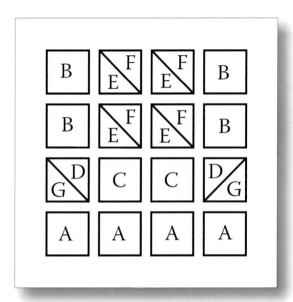

8″ FINISHED BLOCK

(A) Four 2 1/2″ green or blue squares for the water at the bottom ⬜

(B) Four 2 1/2″ blue squares for the sky ⬜

(C) Two 2 1/2″ red squares for the boat ⬜

(D) One 3 7/8″ red square cut on the diagonal ◩

(E) Two 3 7/8″ yellow squares cut on the diagonal ◩

(F) Two 3 7/8″ blue sky print squares cut on the diagonal for the sky against the sails of the ship ◩

(G) One 3 7/8″ green or blue water print square cut on the diagonal bottom sides of the boat ◩

BLOCK PIECING INSTRUCTIONS:

A. Sew your triangles into half-squares.

B. Sew your blocks into rows.

C. Sew the rows into the block.

Press each row's seams in the opposite direction from the row above or below it. The only exception is the center of the sail, where you should carefully pull the stitches out of the seam allowance and press all the seams in one direction clockwise or counter-clockwise (whichever the fabric seems to want to go). This will make the block lay flatter.

Snazzy Store Bought Pillow

Director's Chair Cover

$\mathcal{D}$irector's chairs are very functional chairs that are easy to store away when not needed. They can be even more fun when you customize them with quilt blocks to add that touch of hand-work to an inexpensive store-bought item.

Director's Chair Cover

MATERIALS:
- One or more director's chairs with covers
- One or more 6 ¹/₂″ or smaller quilt blocks for each chair (three 4 ¹/₂″, 4″ finished, friendship star blocks were used in this project)
- Four ¹/₂″ strips to border the blocks with (two 13″ strips and two 4″ strips were used in this project)
- One piece of batting the same size as each quilt block used

INSTRUCTIONS:
A. First decide how many blocks you will be using.
B. If you are following our example, then you will sew three 4″ blocks together into a row.
C. Sew a strip to each side of the block and then one to the top and bottom of the row.
D. Layer the block strip on top of a piece of batting about ¹/₂″ inch smaller than the top and quilt in any way you choose.
E. Fold the strips around to the back like binding and baste in place to the batting.
F. Pin block strip on each side of the back cover of the chair, making sure it is centered and in the same position. Topstitch in place.

FRIENDSHIP STAR BLOCK

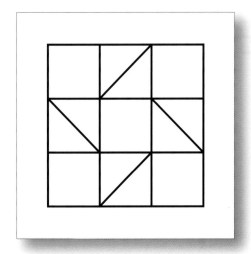

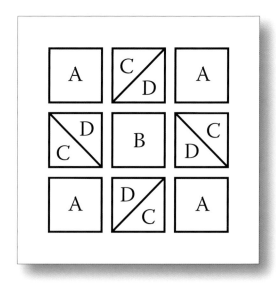

3″ FINISHED BLOCK (MAKE 3 OF THESE)
(A) Four 1¹/₂″ blue water print squares
(B) One 1¹/₂″ yellow print square
(C) Four 1 ⁷/₈″ blue water print squares cut in half on the diagonal
(D) Four 1 ⁷/₈″ yellow print squares cut in half on the diagonal

PIECED BLOCK INSTRUCTIONS:
A. Sew the half-square triangles together.
B. Sew the half-square triangle units and the squares together as a nine-patch as seen in the diagram above.

Dutchman's Puzzle Pillow

$\mathcal{H}$ere is a classic pieced quilt block used in an accent pillow that can add a bit of art to a chair, sofa, or bed. This makes a great gift item, as well.

Dutchman's Puzzle Pillow

MATERIALS:

- One 12 ½" (12" finished) block
- One 16" square pillow form
- ⅓ yard of coordinating fabric for border around block
- ½ yard of coordinating fabric for pillow back (can be same as borders or a different fabric)
- 1 yard of muslin (or any light color "ugly" fabric)
- One 16 ½" square piece of batting
- Two 10" x 16 ½" piece of batting

INSTRUCTIONS:

Assemble pillow face with quilt block

A. Cut two 2 ½" x 12 ½" strips and two 2 ½" x 16 ½" strips of border fabric.

B. Sew the 2 ½" x 12 ½" strips to the side of the quilt block.

C. Sew the 2 ½" x 16 ½" strips to the top and bottom of the quilt block.

D. Cut a 16 ½" square of muslin.

E. Layer the muslin, batting and bordered block. Quilt in any way you choose (the pieces in this project were machine quilted).

Assemble back of pillow case

F. Cut two 10" x 16 ½" pieces of pillow backing fabric and muslin.

G. Layer each 10" x 16 ½" pillow backing fabric with its batting and muslin and quilt.

Make binding for pieces that will be the back of the pillow

H. Cut two 2 ½" x 16 ½" strips of fabric to bind center edges of pillow back pieces so that the back pieces overlap somewhat and help keep the case more securely on the pillow. In this pillow we used the fabric for the pillow back.

I. Sew a strip of binding to one side of each of the two 10" x 16 ½" quilted pieces (see general instructions for making binding).

Stitch together face of pillow with quilt block and pillow backing

J. Lay the quilted block piece face-up and then carefully place the two 10" x 16 ½" pieces with the binding edges overlapping each other face-down at the middle of the pillow, making sure the raw edges of all the pieces are lined up together.

K. Sew a ¼" seam around the whole cover.

L. Turn right-side out and make sure to poke corners out to crisp points. Insert pillow form.

DUTCHMAN'S PUZZLE BLOCK

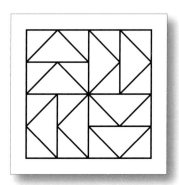

12" FINISHED BLOCK

(A) One 7 ¼" lavender print square from one print fabric, cut twice on the diagonal to yield four triangles per square

(B) One 7 ¼" blue print square from another fabric, cut twice on the diagonal to yield four triangles per square

(C) Eight 3 ⅞" green print squares, cut them once on the diagonal to yield two triangles per square

BLOCK PIECING INSTRUCTIONS:

A. Sew eight sets of two small triangles to one large triangle, pressing the seams toward the darkest fabric.

B. Sew four sets of two of the units pieced above together so that you have four 6 ½" squares, pressing the seams toward the bottoms of the larger triangles.

C. Sew the four squares together, pressing the seams toward the bottoms of the triangles again.

Little Piped Pillow

This is a cute little pillow to accent any room. Make it with extra blocks from a quilt you have made, and the matching, piped pillow will give your bed a very finished look. This particular pillow was made with a "reject" block from an anniversary quilt.

Little Piped Pillow

MATERIALS:

- One quilt block of any size: (A 10 1/2″ block, 10″ finished, was used in this project)
- 1/4 yard piece of coordinating fabric for borders: (In this project we used two 1/8 yards of two different fabrics for borders)
- One fat quarter of coordinating fabric to make a cover for the piping
- One 54″ piece of size 4/32″ cording
- One bag polyester stuffing or a pillow form the size of your finished cover

INSTRUCTIONS:

Pillow Face and Piping

A. Cut 1″ strips out of the 1/4 yard piece of fabric.

B. Sew a strip to each side of the block and then a strip to the top and the bottom of the block.

C. Cut 1 1/4″ strips on the bias for the piping. Sew the strips together and wrap around the cording to make piping.

Assemble backing, piping and pillow face with block

D. Cut a 13″ piece of backing fabric.

E. Lay the quilt block face-up and then lay the piping around the outer edge with the piping facing the inside and the raw edges facing out. Place the backing face-down on top and pin in place.

Stitching backing, piping and face together and finishing

F. Begin on one side of the pillow cover and sew a 1/4″ seam all around the cover, stopping about 4″ from where you started. Make sure to sew right up close to the edge of the piping. The closer to the piping the stitching is the better it will look.

G. Turn right-side out through the 4″ opening and stuff with the stuffing.

H. Sew the opening shut with a blind-hem stitch, making sure to catch the piping in the stitches.

SQUARE WITH BORDERS BLOCK

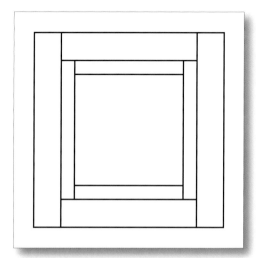

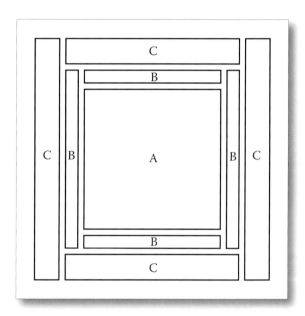

8″ FINISHED BLOCK

(A) One 7″ pink dot square of fabric

(B) Four 1″ x 8″ purple dot strips

(C) Four 2″ x 10″ pink strips

BLOCK PIECING INSTRUCTIONS:

A. Sew the 1″ strips to the top and bottom of the square first and then the side strips.

B. Sew the 2″ strips to the top and bottom of the square first and then the side strips.

Magazine Wall Hanging

$\mathcal{D}$o you ever find that you have an unmanageable stack of books and magazines on your bed-side table? This project will give you a new organizational tool for magazines while also giving you a neat quilted piece of artwork for your wall.

Magazine Wallhanging

MATERIALS:

- Two 12 ½″ (12″ finished) quilt blocks
- Two 15″ square pieces of backing fabric for your blocks
- Two 15″ square pieces of batting or flannel
- Eight 2″ x 12 ½″ strips of coordinating fabric
- Two 25″ x 36″ pieces of coordinating fabric
- One 25″ x 36″ piece of batting
- 4 yards of bias binding

INSTRUCTIONS:

Border the Blocks, Layer and Stitch Closed

A. Border each 12 ½″ block with the 2″ x 12 ½″ strips to make each block 14 ½″.

B. Layer one piece of batting with a piece of backing fabric face-up and the 14 ½″ bordered quilt block face-down. Starting on one side, sew a ¼″ seam all the way around each block leaving a 5″ opening where you started. Trim the edges neatly, trim the corners and then turn right-side out. Poke corners out so they are crisp. Stitch the openings up with a blind-hem stitch. Repeat this process with the second quilt block.

Back of magazine wall hanging and topstitching quilt blocks

C. Layer the two 25″ x 36″ pieces of backing fabric with the same sized batting in between and quilt in any manner you choose.

D. Pin the two quilt blocks to the center of the quilted piece, one above the other. Topstitch down one side, along the bottom, and up the other side of each block, leaving the top open to allow for magazines to slide into the pockets.

Finish by binding

E. Machine-sew the binding onto the right-side of the background quilt and then wrap around to the back side to hand-sew to the back using a blind-hem stitch.

Optional:

You can make two hanging sleeves for the back of this project, one behind the top of each pocket to support the back when heavy magazines are in the pocket.

MATERIALS:

- Two 8″ x 20″ strips of fabric

Optional Hanging Sleeve Instructions:

A. Sew a ½″ double-fold seam on the two sides of each piece so it becomes 8″ x 18″.

B. Fold each piece in half lengthwise with the right sides together and sew together with a ½″ seam.

C. Turn right-side out, press flat with the seam in the middle of one side, and sew to the upper back and the middle of the quilt using a blind-hem stitch at the top and bottom of the fabric tube.

CHURN DASH BLOCK

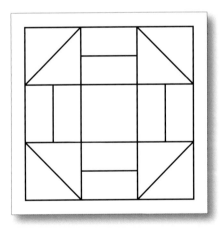

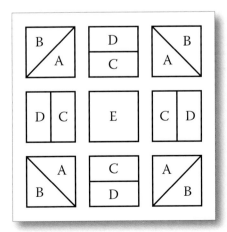

12″ FINISHED BLOCK

(A) Two red 4 $^7/_8$″ squares cut in half on the diagonal

(B) Two white 4 $^7/_8$″ squares cut in half on the diagonal

(C) Four orange 4 $^1/_2$″ x 2 $^1/_2$″ rectangles

(D) Four white 4 $^1/_2$″ x 2 $^1/_2$″ rectangles

(E) One novelty print 4 $^1/_2$″ square

BLOCK PIECING INSTRUCTIONS:

I. Sew the pairs of red and white triangles and the pairs of orange and white rectangles together as seen in the diagram opposite. Press the seams here towards the darker fabric.

J. Piece the sewn blocks into three rows and then the rows into a nine-patch to get the finished block.

K. When piecing the blocks into their rows, press the top and bottom rows' seams towards the center and the middle row's seams towards the outside.

L. When piecing the rows together, press the row seams towards the center row.

BEARS PAW BLOCK

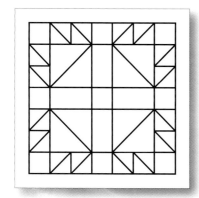

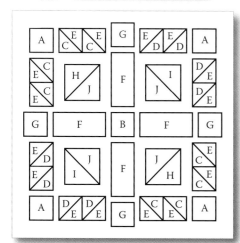

12″ FINISHED BLOCK

(A) Four white 2 $^1/_4$″ squares

(B) One orange print 2 $^1/_4$″ square

(C) Four blue print squares 2 $^5/_8$″ cut in half on the diagonal

(D) Four novelty print squares 2 $^5/_8$″ cut in half on the diagonal

(E) Eight white 2 $^5/_8$″ squares cut in half on the diagonal

(F) Four yellow 2 $^1/_4$″ x 3 $^7/_8$″ rectangles

(G) Four red 2 $^1/_4$″ squares

(H) One blue print 4 $^3/_4$″ square cut in half on the diagonal

(I) One novelty print 4 $^3/_4$″ square cut in half on the diagonal

(J) Two white 4 $^3/_4$″ square cut in half on the diagonal

BLOCK PIECING INSTRUCTIONS:

A. Sew the two larger blue and novelty print triangles each to a white triangle of the same size to make the 3 $^7/_8$″ squares needed for step G.

B. Sew the 2 $^1/_4$″ orange center square to two of the yellow colored rectangles and then sew a red square to each end of these strips.

C. Sew a red square to an end of the other two yellow rectangles.

D. Sew pairs of white & blue and white & novelty print triangles together to make eight of each half-square units.

E. Sew these half-square units into four sets of two blocks of each set of fabric.

F. Sew four of the pairs (of two blocks sewn together) to a white square so that you have four rows of three blocks and four rows of two blocks.

G. Sew the rows of two blocks to the 3 $^7/_8$″ squares and then sew the three block rows to one side as seen in the diagram.

H. Sew two pairs of paws together with a yellow and red rectangle unit in between and then sew the three rows together.

Quilter's Seat Cushion

$\mathcal{Q}$uilters like to have a comfortable seat when they are going to be sewing for awhile. Many take a seat cushion along to classes with them. What better seat cushion to have than a quilted seat cushion.

Quilter's Seat Cushion

MATERIALS:

- **One 12 $\frac{1}{2}$″ (12″ finished) quilt block (this project uses a saw-tooth star).**
- **Two 3 $\frac{1}{2}$″ x 12 $\frac{1}{2}$″ strips cut from a coordinating fabric**
- **Two 2 $\frac{1}{2}$″ x 17 $\frac{1}{2}$″ strips cut from a coordinating fabric**
- **One piece of coordinating fabric 17″ x 19″**
- **Two pieces of muslin 17″ x 19″ (or any fabric you don't like or aren't using)**
- **Two pieces of batting 17″ x 19″**
- **One 16″ x 18″ piece of 1″ foam**
- **Four 15″ pieces of straight-grain binding or ribbon for ties**

INSTRUCTIONS:

A. Sew the 3 $\frac{1}{2}$″ x 12 $\frac{1}{2}$″ strip to the side of the quilt block. Trim the ends of the strips even with the edge of the block.

B. Next sew the 2 $\frac{1}{2}$″ x 17 $\frac{1}{2}$″ strips to the top and bottom. Trim the edges of these strips, as well.

C. Layer the backing, batting and top for quilting and quilt in the manner you choose.

D. Layer the backing piece of the seat cushion with its batting and backing and quilt as above.

Assembling cover for cushion

E. Layer the top piece of the cushion with the block face-up and the backing piece of the seat cushion cover face-down.

F. Pin the ties into the seam toward the back corners of the cushion cover so the ties are lying inside the two pieces of the cushion cover.

G. Stitch these pieces together starting on the back of the cover with a $\frac{1}{2}$″ seam allowance and stopping about 10″ from where you started on the back-side to leave an opening for turning. Make sure to catch the ties in the seam.

H. Turn the cushion cover right-side out. Measure your cover to see the final size and trim the foam to a $\frac{1}{4}$″ smaller than the size of the cushion cover. Stuff the piece of foam into the cover working with it until the cushion lies flat.

I. Finish by hand sewing the opening closed with a blind-hem stitch.

SAW TOOTH STAR BLOCK

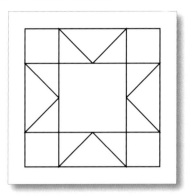

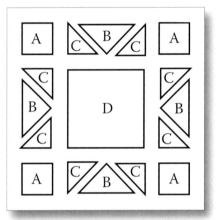

12″ FINISHED BLOCK

(A) **Four pink print 3 $\frac{1}{2}$″ squares**

(B) **One pink print 7 $\frac{1}{2}$″ square cut in half twice on the diagonal**

(C) **Four blue print 3 $\frac{7}{8}$ squares cut in half once on the diagonal**

(D) **One green print 6 $\frac{1}{2}$″ square**

BLOCK PIECING INSTRUCTIONS:

A. Sew the four sets of triangles together, pressing the seams towards the darker fabric.

B. Sew a triangle set to each side of the center square, pressing the seams towards the center square.

C. Sew squares to the ends of the other two triangle sets, pressing the seams towards the outer squares. Sew these two rows to the top and bottom of the center row, pressing the seams towards the top and bottom rows.

Quilter's Seat Cushion

Sewing Machine Cover

$\mathcal{D}$o you keep a sewing machine up all the time, or at least a good bit of time when you're in the middle of a project? Do you have a friend or relative who uses a sewing machine and keeps it out? Use a pieced quilt block or two, choose fabric you like and make this unique and fun sewing machine cover. This is a great way to protect the machine from dust and dirt when it's not in use, makes the sewing corner look neater, and makes a work of art out of a practical tool to cover the machine.

Sewing Machine Cover

MATERIALS:

- **One or two 8 $\frac{1}{2}''$ (8″ finished) quilt blocks (the cover pictured here uses an 8 inch spool block)**
- **One or two 8 $\frac{1}{2}''$ coordinating backing blocks for your pieced blocks**
- **One or two 8 $\frac{1}{2}''$ pieces of thin cotton batting**
  Note: An alternative is to piece the blocks into the fabric that you use for the outside of your cover. With this method you would not need backing and batting for the blocks.
- **1 yard of main background fabric for the outside of the cover**
- **1 yard lining fabric for the underside of the cover**
- **1 yard thin cotton batting**
- **$\frac{3}{4}$ yard of fabric for to use for binding, or purchase binding in a color that coordinates or with the cover fabric**

INSTRUCTIONS:

Make three important measurements, first.

A. Measure the width across the top and bottom of the sewing machine. (this measurement should be about 17″ - 20″ depending on the type of machine).

B. Measure the height of your machine (the measurement should be about 13″ - 16″) and the depth of your machine from front to back (the measurement should be about 10″ - 13″).

C. The last measurement you need is from the bottom of one side of your machine over the top and down the other side. Think in terms of an upside-down U shape (the measurement should be about 42″ - 46″).

Note: If you choose to piece your blocks into the cover then you should first subtract the size of your quilt block from the overall measurement you need for the sides of your toaster. Divide the remaining width and height by two to get the size of strips you need to add to the blocks to get your side panels. You will need to add about $\frac{1}{2}''$ to each strip to allow for seam allowances. Then cut your batting and lining fabric accordingly.

Make pieced quilt blocks for decorating the cover.

D. Layer together two 8″ blocks with the batting first, the backing face-up next and the pieced block face-down last.

E. Begin in the middle of one side, sewing around the outer edge of the block, leaving a 2 $\frac{1}{2}''$ opening where you began through which the blocks are turned right side out.

F. Turn your blocks right-side out and poke out the corners. Fold in the fabric and batting at the opening and iron in preparation for sewing shut. Set these aside for the next step.

Cut pieces for the cover

G. Cut out the three pieces of the main background fabric for the outside, the pieces of lining and the pieces of batting. The size will be determined by the three measurements you made.
   Note: if you plan to use quilt blocks as pockets stitched to the outside of the cover, you can simplify at this step by layering the whole piece of main background fabric, the lining fabric and the batting. If you are piecing the blocks into the cover fabric then you will need to follow the note mentioned for measuring and then sew the blocks and border strips into the pieces that you will use for your cover pieces.

H. Layer each set of lining pieces and outer pieces of fabric with batting and quilt in any manner you choose.

Attach blocks to each of the two side panels.

I. Pin a quilted block to each of the two side panels, or the front and back panel, for the cover, making sure that the opening is pinned and facing down.

Sewing Machine Cover

J. Top-stitch the quilt blocks to their cover pieces, making sure that the seam allowance of the opening in the blocks is caught in the top-stitching.

Bind and assemble the pieces into a cover

K. Make or buy 4 ½ yards of bias binding.

L. Pin the binding and front panel of your cover to the long top panel matching up the front panel and top panel at one corner to start your sewing and then stitch together with the seam on the outside of the cover.

M. Follow the same instructions with the back panel, starting at the same end as the front. Trim off any extra fabric on the top panel at the one end. Fold the binding over the seams and hand-sew on with a blind-hem stitch.

N. Machine-sew the binding on the outside bottom edge of the cover and fold over to hand-sew the binding on the inside of the cover.

Suggestions for quilting:

A nice machine quilting pattern for these covers is to quilt about 2″ apart in diagonal lines that cross each other so that you have a diamond pattern. This also works well with spray basting to make it even easier.

Depending on the fabrics chosen for the cover, a nice effect can be achieved if you hand quilt, and using a pattern that accentuates the pattern in your fabric.

SPOOL BLOCK

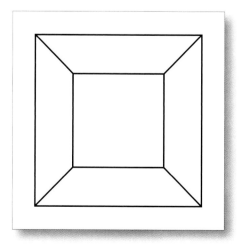

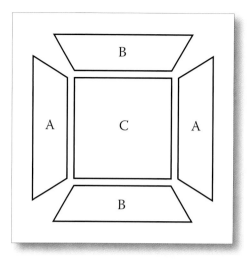

8″ BLOCK

(A) Two 2 ½″ x 9 ¼″ rectangles in novelty print. Place them right-sides together and cut a 45° angle cut off each end

(B) Two light brown 2 ½″ x 9 ¼″ rectangles cut in the same manner as above

(C) One 4 ½″ square in a striped fabric to look like thread on a spool

BLOCK PIECING INSTRUCTIONS:

A. Sew the two novelty print borders on opposite sides of the center square, starting and stopping ¼″ from the beginning and the end.

B. Sew the two light brown borders on the other two sides of the square in the same manner as above.

C. Fold the block in half on the diagonal lining up the raw angled cut edges of the border strips and sew from the corner point out to the edge back-stitching at the beginning and the end.

TOTES AND BAGS

So, you have lots of goodies to carry to your kid's school or your quilting class next week. Maybe you need something to organize your needles or computer discs. Add quilted style totes and organizers and be the envy of all your friends.

Shannon's Tote

$\int$ ome craft stores carry very inexpensive light-weight canvas totes that are really fun to embellish with fabric dye and quilt blocks. You can have fun with this bag.

Shannon's Tote

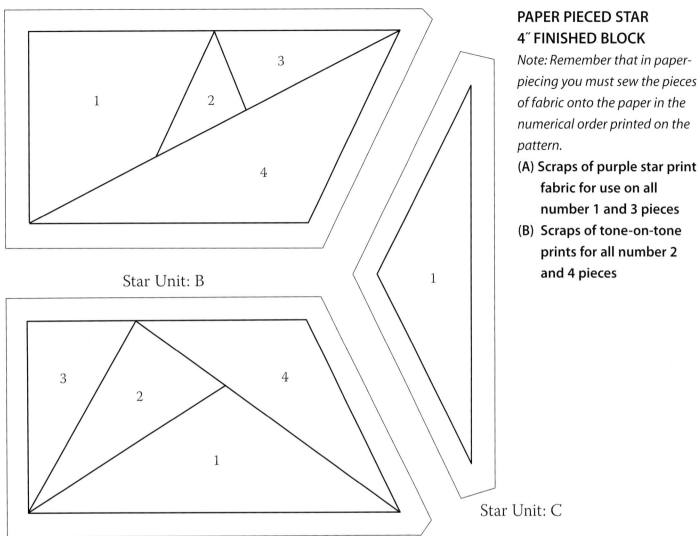

Star Unit: A

Star Unit: B

Star Unit: C

**PAPER PIECED STAR
4″ FINISHED BLOCK**

Note: Remember that in paper-piecing you must sew the pieces of fabric onto the paper in the numerical order printed on the pattern.

(A) Scraps of purple star print fabric for use on all number 1 and 3 pieces

(B) Scraps of tone-on-tone prints for all number 2 and 4 pieces

MATERIALS:

- One or more store-bought light-weight canvas bags
- One package of good quality fabric dye in each color you choose
- A nice selection of fabric scraps
- Several different small quilt block patterns all the same size (4 ¹/₂″, 4″ finished, blocks were used in this pattern)
- Two beads
- Embroidery floss
- Small scrap for nose

INSTRUCTIONS:

A. Following the directions on the package of dye, dye the tote to the desired shade.

B. Measure the width of the bag and double for the measurement around the whole bag.

C. Divide the bag measurement taken above by the size of your finished blocks to find out how many blocks you need. You may not come out with a round number so you will have to add a few strips in between blocks or at the joining ends of the strip to make the strip the right size.

D. Make the number of blocks that you need and sew them together side to side to form a long strip.

E. Turn a ¹/₂″ of the top and bottom of the pieced strip in towards the wrong side and press the fold into place.

F. Pin the strip into place on the bag 2″ - 4″ from the top and topstitch right at the edges of the top and the bottom of the strip.

Shannon's Tote

Heart

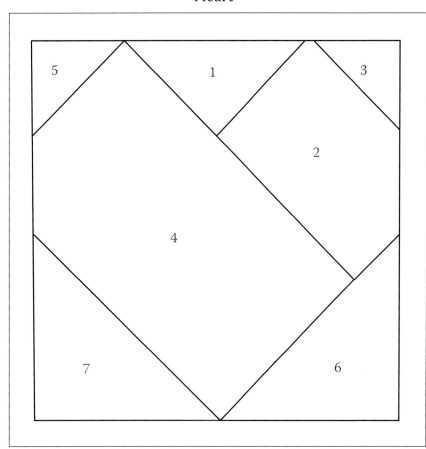

PAPER PIECED HEART
4″ FINISHED BLOCK

Note: Remember that in paper-piecing you must sew the pieces of fabric onto the paper in the numerical order printed on the pattern.

(A) Scraps of red fabric for use on numbers 2 and 4 pieces

(B) Scraps of orange batik for numbers 1, 3 and 5-7 pieces

PAPER PIECED FLOWER
4″ FINISHED BLOCK

Note: Remember that in paper-piecing you must sew the pieces of fabric onto the paper in the numerical order printed on the pattern.

(A) Scraps of pink hand-dyed fabric for use on numbers 1-8 pieces

(B) Scraps of green hand-dyed fabric for numbers 9-14 pieces

(E) Scraps of green for leaves (optional - instructions on page 85)

Flower

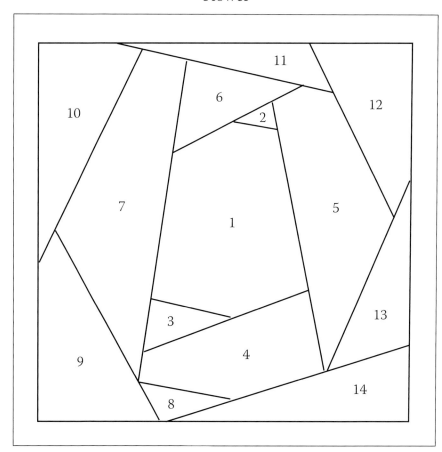

Shannon's Tote

Cat

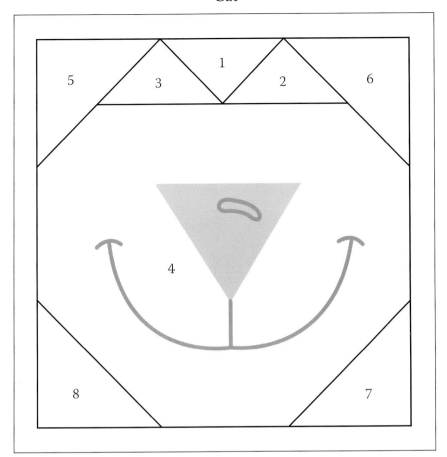

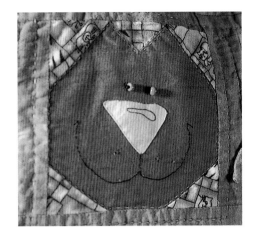

PAPER PIECED CAT
4˝ FINISHED BLOCK

Note: Remember that in paper-piecing you must sew the pieces of fabric onto the paper in the numerical order printed on the pattern.

(A) Scraps of brown fabric for use on numbers 2, 3, and 4 pieces

(B) Scraps of pastel print fabric for numbers 1 and 5-8 pieces

(C) Small triangle of light pink fabric for nose

(D) Two green beads for eyes

(E) Black thread for embroidered mouth and nose

OPTIONAL LEAVES FOR FLOWER

(A) Using templates for the leaves, cut two leaf pieces for each template

(B) Place the two matching leaf pieces right-sides together and stitch around the outside with a 1 ¼˝ seam, leaving an opening to turn right-side out

(C) Place one leaf into seam when adding the number 10 and 13 pieces to the block

(D) After the block is finished you can, if you choose, sew the leaves down to the block to keep them from flapping

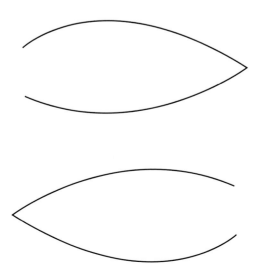

Canvas Tote

$\mathcal{D}$o you have an abundance of those commercially printed canvas bags that are given out at store openings, conferences and other events? I have some of these I don't want to carry because of the advertising on the sides. In this project we have recycled one of these bags and covered the advertising with interesting quilt blocks in a coordinating color.

Canvas Tote

MATERIALS:

- One canvas tote (you will love this so much you may need many more totes to recycle!)
- One or two 8 $1/2$" - 12 $1/2$" ($1/2$" smaller finished) quilt blocks. The size of the blocks depends on your bag, (this project uses a 10 $1/2$" block)
- One fat quarter of a coordinating fabric for binding and pockets
- A piece of batting for each block that is about the same size as the block or blocks you are using for this project

INSTRUCTIONS:

A. Cut four 1" strips for each block from the fat quarter.

B. Sew a strip to each side of the block and then one to the top and bottom of the block.

C. Center the batting on the back of the block and quilt in the ditch around the piecing in the block.

D. Fold the strips around to the back, like binding, and baste in place to the batting.

E. Topstitch the block in place to cover the advertising on the bag or hand-sew with a blind-hem stitch.

F. Optional step: pockets on the inside of the bag (see below).

OPTIONAL STEP:

Make smaller pockets to go inside the bag to organize smaller things you carry in a tote.

A. Layer smaller blocks with the batting first, then the back face-up and the block face-down.

B. Sew the three layers together leaving an opening in the side in order to turn the block right-side out.

C. After turning, finish the block by hand or machine sewing the opening closed. You can use these smaller finished blocks as pockets on the inside of the bag by topstitching or hand-sewing the two sides and the bottom of the block to the inside of the bag. Leave the top open and unstitched so you can use it as a pocket.

If you choose to add this step, put the pockets inside the bag before topstitching the outside decoration blocks to the canvass tote.

DUTCHMAN'S PUZZLE BLOCK

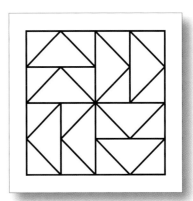

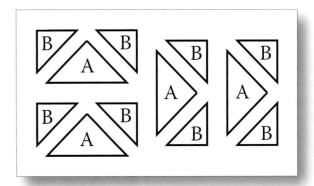

12" FINISHED BLOCK

(A) Two pink & blue batik stripe 7 $1/4$" squares, cut twice on the diagonal to yield four triangles per square

(B) Eight brown batik 3 $7/8$" squares, cut once on the diagonal to yield two triangles per square

BLOCK PIECING INSTRUCTIONS:

A. Sew eight sets of two small triangles to one large triangle, pressing the seams toward the dark fabric.

B. Sew four sets of two of the units pieced above together so that you have four 6 $1/2$" squares, pressing the seams toward the bottoms of the larger triangles.

C. Sew the four squares together, pressing the seams toward the bottoms of the triangles again.

Quilter's Tool Bag

$\mathcal{T}$his is the perfect bag for carrying your large cutting mat and rulers to class. The measurements included here are for an 18″ x 24″ cutting mat, but you can make it any size you need to accommodate your cutting mat. It's nice for this bag to be a little snug to support your cutting mat and rulers.

Quilter's Tool Bag

MATERIALS:

- **Two 24″ x 40″ pieces of the same fabric or two complementary fabrics for the main part of the bag**
- **One or two 12 ½″ (12″ finished) blocks for the pockets**
- **One or two 12 ½″ pieces of backing fabric for the blocks**
- **One or two 12 ½″ pieces of very thin batting or flannel**
- **3 - 4 yards of belting in a coordinating color**
- **One 24″ x 40″ piece of cotton batting**

INSTRUCTIONS:

A. The first step in construction is to lay out the batting, then one piece of fabric face-up and the next face-down. Start sewing on one side and sew all the way around the sandwich stopping about 5″ from where you started. Trim off the corners of your sewn sandwiches and then turn them right side out. You can hand sew the opening up or can top-stitch it closed.

B. You can quilt this piece at this point (and should if you use batting that needs to be quilted close together).

C. Next sew each 12 ½″ block and 12 ½″ piece of backing fabric right sides together with a very thin piece of batting or a piece of flannel, leaving a 5″ opening in one side and turn right-side out in the same manner as above.

D. Lay the large quilted piece out first and then pin the two blocks to the sides of your bag, centering them in the middle from side to side and making sure they are not too close to the top edges of the bag or to the bottom fold of the bag. Topstitch the bottom edge of each block (closest to the fold of the bag) to the bag to make the bottom edge of the pockets (the side edges will be attached to the bag in the next step).

E. Next lay the belting as shown in the diagram in an oval with a loop hanging off each end of the big piece (as much as you want your handles to be) and the two ends meeting in the middle (bottom of bag), making sure the belting covers the edges of the blocks.

F. Stitch two rows of stitches down the length of the belting to secure the belting to the bag making sure to catch the pocket in the stitch.

G. Fold bag in half with right-sides facing each other and sew up the sides using a ½″ seam allowance.

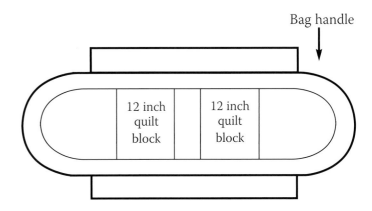

Bag handle

Instructions continued on page 91.

OLD MAID'S PUZZLE BLOCK

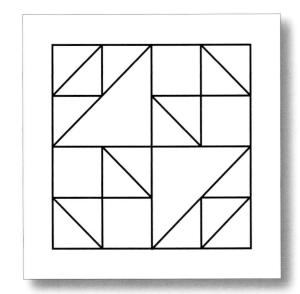

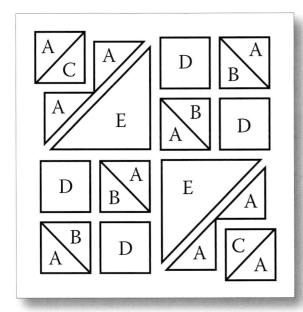

12″ FINISHED BLOCK

(A) **Five black 3 ⅞″ squares cut in half once on the diagonal** ◹

(B) **Two plaid 3 ⅞″ squares cut in half once on the diagonal** ◹

(C) **One orange dot 3 ⅞″ square cut in half once on the diagonal** ◹

(D) **Four black 3 ½″ squares** □

(E) **One orange dot 6 ⅞″ square cut in half once on the diagonal** ◹

BLOCK PIECING INSTRUCTIONS:

A. Sew all the half square triangle units together, pressing the seams toward the darker fabric.

B. Sew two black triangles to the corner half-square units to make a larger triangle, pressing the seams toward the darker fabric.

C. Sew the pieced large triangles to the large orange dot triangles to make two of the pieced squares for the final four-patch, pressing toward the larger triangles.

D. Sew two sets of two half-square units to two black squares in a four-patch to make the other set of pieced squares that make of the final four-patch, pressing the seams in the opposite direction from each other.

E. Sew the final four blocks together in the order seen in the diagram above, pressing towards the larger triangles.

Trick-or-Treat Bag

Every child loves Halloween. This special tote is just
the trick to bring home all those treats.

Trick-or-Treat Bag

MATERIALS:

- One 12 ½″ (12″ finished) quilt block (a house block is used for this project)
- One 12 ½″ piece of backing fabric for the block
- One 12 ½″ piece of light-weight cotton batting
- Two different coordinating pieces of Halloween print fabric 24″ x 36″
- 3 yards of coordinating belting cut into two equal pieces
- Thread in coordinating color for topstitching

INSTRUCTIONS:

Quilt Block

A. Layer the batting, backing face-up and the pieced block face-down last.

B. Begin stitching in the middle of one side with a ¼″ seam allowance leaving a 5″ hole where you began stitching. Trim the edges and corners neatly.

C. Turn the block right-side out and poke out the corners so they are crisp and sharp.

D. Fold in the fabric and batting at the hole and iron in preparation for sewing shut. Set aside for the next step.

Trick or Treat Bag

E. Fold each 24″ x 36″ piece of fabric with right-sides together in half so it ends up 24″ x 18″.

F. Sew each piece across the bottom and up the side so that with the fold on one side and stitching on two sides each piece is now a bag shape.

G. Turn the bag made with fabric you want on the outside bag right-side out.

H. Fit the fabric that is to be inside the bag down into the outside bag. The right side of one fabric is the inside of the bag and the right side of one piece of fabric is on the outside with the wrong sides of these fabrics facing each other.

I. Fold the tops of each bag down towards their wrong-sides about 1 ½″ so that the tops of both are equal height.

J. Pin around the top and topstitch with two rows of stitching, one right up at the top and one about 1″ below the top in a coordinating thread color.

Attach quilt block and handles to complete this bag.

K. Pin the quilt block that you set aside earlier to the center of one side of the bag.

L. Pin the belting to the bag so that one piece starts just below the bottom of the quilt block and so it covers the side of the block. Curve the belting up above the bag and bring it back down the opposite side of the block covering the edge of the block. Pin the other piece of belting to the back side of the bag in the same place.

M. Topstitch each piece of belting to the bag on both sides of the belting so that it is securely sewn to the bag.

HOUSE BLOCK

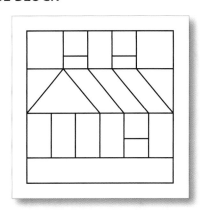

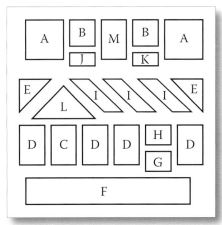

12″ FINISHED BLOCK

(A) Two blue sky 3 ½″ squares

(B) Two blue sky 2 ½″ squares

(C) One focus print (an animal to look out the door) 2 ½″ x 3 ½″ rectangle

(D) Four 2 ½″ x 3 ½″ inch rectangles of fabric for the front of the house

Trick-or-Treat Bag

(E) Two blue sky fabric 3 ³/₄″ x 4 ³/₈″ placed right-sides together and then cut in half once on the diagonal (You will use only two of the triangles, but have to cut four to get the right direction)

(F) One green grass 3″ x 12 ¹/₂″ rectangle

(G) One 2″ x 2 ¹/₂″ rectangle, the same fabric as the front of the house

(H) One 2″ x 2 ¹/₂″ rectangle, a focus print (an animal to look out the window)

(I) Three purple prints of template A

(J) One purple print 1 ¹/₂″ x 2 ¹/₂″ rectangle

(K) One blue sky print 1 ¹/₂″ x 2 ¹/₂″ rectangle

(L) One purple print of template B

(M) One blue sky print 2 ¹/₂″ x 3 ¹/₂″ rectangle

BLOCK PIECING INSTRUCTIONS:

A. Sew the smaller rectangles together from the second and top rows. See diagrams opposite.

B. Sew all the pieces in a row together to make the three pieced rows, pressing the seams in the second and top rows one way and the seams in the third row the opposite way.

C. Sew the four rows together, pressing the seams where they want to go.

Note: The blocks used in the Trick-or-Treat bag are paper-pieced blocks. See the general instructions for more information on paper-piecing. Copy each pattern piece the exact size and sew your pieces of fabric in numeric order to the back side of the pattern. Then tear the paper off the back of the block.

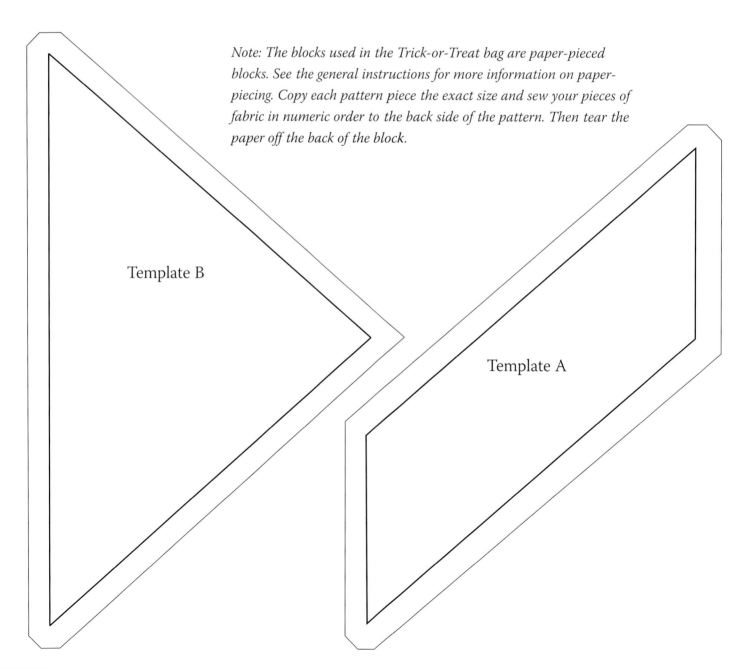

Template B

Template A

Origami Purse

Every quilter should have a variety of quilted purses to show off their artistry when they're out and about town. This is a beautiful purse that is fairly easy to make and very versatile. Be warned, your non-quilting friends will want you to make them one!

Origami Purse

MATERIALS:

- **One 6 $\frac{1}{2}$" (6" finished) quilt block**
- **$\frac{1}{2}$ yard of coordinating fabric for front, sides and bottom of bag**
- **$\frac{1}{2}$ yard of coordinating fabric for back of bag**
- **$\frac{3}{4}$ yard of coordinating fabric for lining of bag**
- **Two 13" x 15" pieces of fabric for inside pockets**
- **$\frac{1}{2}$ yard fabric for bias binding or 3 yards of ready-made binding**
- **Cotton batting**
- **$\frac{1}{8}$ yard fabric for block borders and scraps for corner stones (a turquoise print and a rust oriental print were used here)**

Note: All raw edges will be covered with bias binding. When piecing, be sure to remember to sew with wrong sides together. All seams are sewn using a $\frac{1}{4}$" seam allowance, unless otherwise noted.

INSTRUCTIONS:

A. Cut four 1 $\frac{1}{2}$" x 6 $\frac{1}{2}$" strips from the $\frac{1}{8}$ yard and four 1 $\frac{1}{2}$" squares from the scraps. Sew two of the borders to the block and the other two to their two corner stones and then to the block.

B. Cut four 4" x 22" strips and three 4" x 16" strips from the fabric you will use for the front, sides and bottom of bag

C. Cut one 16" x 16" square from the fabric you will use for the back of the bag

D. Cut three 4" x 16" strips and two 16" x16" squares from the fabric you will use for the lining of the bag.

E. Sew the four 4" x 22" strips that you will be using for the outside of the tote bag to the bordered block, being sure to miter the corners (you can also sew strips straight across if desired). This will make the front of tote bag.

F. Layer a 16" x 16" piece of batting behind the piece that will be used as the front of bag and quilt in any way you choose.

G. Layer the 16" x 16" piece of fabric that will be used for back of tote on top of a 16" x 16" piece

of batting. Quilt the two pieces in any way you choose (you could sew an X across the back, for example).

H. Fold the 13" x 15 " pieces of fabric in half to make 6 $\frac{1}{2}$" x 16" pieces of fabric.

I. Place each 6 $\frac{1}{2}$" x 16" piece of fabric on top of one of the 16" x 16" squares used for the lining of the bag, lining up the raw edges. Sew a line from the top middle of the folded piece to the bottom of the folded piece on each side. These will become inside pockets for the tote.

J. Place a 4" x 16" piece of batting behind each of the three 4" x 16" strips used for the outside, sides and bottom of bag. Sew lengthwise down the middle of the strip to secure pieces.

K. Layer together front of bag and one 16" x 16" piece of the lining, being sure to keep pockets facing up. Do the same for the back, bottom and sides of tote.

L. Sew front of tote to one 4" x 16" strip used for bottom of tote. Sew back of tote to other side of bottom of tote.

M. Sew remaining 4" x 16" pieces to make sides of tote.

N. Cut 2 $\frac{1}{2}$" strips of bias binding. Fold in half and press. Sew binding down each side of tote. Fold over to the other side and sew down with a blind-hem stitch.

O. Sew another piece of binding to the bottom of the tote. Sew bottom binding to edge of binding coming down side of tote. Remove from sewing machine and wrap around to side of tote. Sew binding to side of tote. Continue until you have sewn binding around bottom of tote. Fold over to the other side and sew down with a blind-hem stitch, being sure to miter the binding at the corners of the tote. Be sure to blind-hem stitch around top of binding where it wraps around sides.

P. Sew a piece of binding to the top of tote. Fold over to the other side and sew down with a blind-hem stitch.

Origami Purse

Q. Cut four 2″ x 22″ pieces of fabric for tote handles. Sandwich together with strips of batting the same size and sew all edges with bias binding.

R. Topstitch the straps on with a coordinating thread in an "x" pattern right below the edge of the binding for reinforcement.

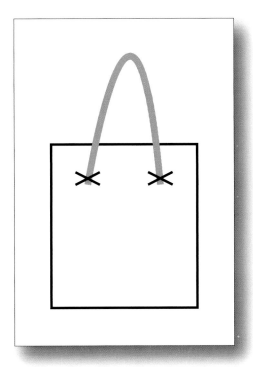

ORIGAMI BLOCK

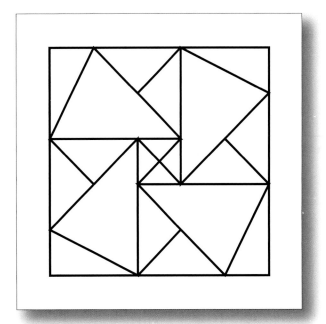

6″ FINISHED BLOCK
- **Make four copies of pattern A**
- **Make one copy each of pattern E and pattern F**
- **(A) A fat quarter of black-on-black print (1,4)**
- **(B) One 12″ piece of rust oriental print (3)**
- **(C) One 12″ piece of gold print (2)**

BORDERS FOR BLOCK
- **1/8 yard turquoise print**
- **5″ square rust oriental print**

See instructions on page 95, section A.

Note: The block used in Origami purse is paper-pieced. See the general instructions for more information on paper-piecing. Copy each pattern piece the exact size and sew your pieces of fabric in numeric order to the back side of the pattern. Then tear the paper off the back of the block.

Origami Purse

Origami A

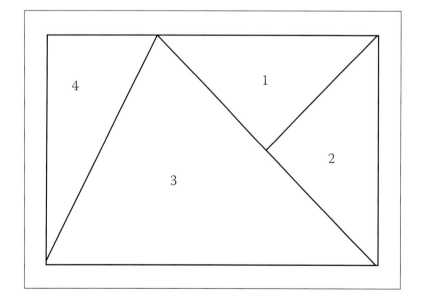

Origami E

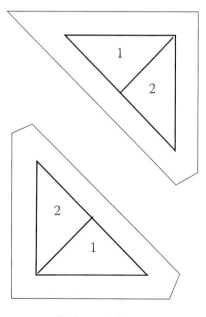

Origami F

Fun Fleece Scarf

$\mathcal{D}$o you just love to wear scarves in the winter to keep you warm? Polyester fleece makes a very warm and comfortable scarf and it's made even better by embellishing it with a quilt block. The quilt block can also be made into a useful part of the scarf by only topstitching the top and bottom to the scarf, leaving the sides open to be used as type of pocket to slide the opposite end of the scarf into to keep the scarf in place.

Fun Fleece Scarf

MATERIALS:
- One 10″ x 60″ piece of polyester fleece
- One 8 ¹/₂″ (8″ finished) pieced quilt block
- One 8 ¹/₂″ square of coordinating fabric to back the block with
- 1 yard of 1 ¹/₂″ bias binding

INSTRUCTIONS:
A. Make 2″ deep cuts every 1″ on the two ends of the piece of fleece.

B. Layer the backing piece face-down and the pieced block face-up and quilt in any way you choose.

C. Machine-sew the binding to the top of the quilted block and then turn over to the back to hand-sew.

D. Drape the scarf around your neck so that the ends are hanging evenly and put a pin in one of the ends of the scarf where it hangs in front of your chest.

E. Pin the quilt block onto the scarf at the level of the pin so that the top and bottom of the block are pinned, but the sides are left un-pinned.

F. Drape the scarf around your neck again and put the opposite end of the scarf through the sides of the pinned quilt block so that the pinned block holds the scarf around your neck.

G. Adjust the level of the quilt block so that the scarf is comfortable around your neck.

H. When you are sure of the placement of the block, top-stitch the top and bottom of the block, just on the inside of the binding strips, to the scarf. Make sure to leave the sides of the block un-stitched so that you can put the opposite end of the scarf through the pocket the block makes, which will hold the scarf in place around your neck.

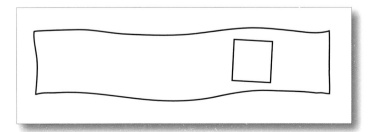

Diagram shows placement of block on scarf.

SAW-TOOTH STAR BLOCK

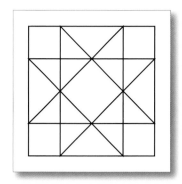
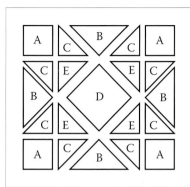

8″ FINISHED BLOCK
(A) Four pink 2 ¹/₂″ squares

(B) One brown 5 ¹/₂″ square cut in half twice on the diagonal

(C) Four blue 2 ⁷/₈″ squares cut in half once on the diagonal

(D) One purple print 3 ³/₈″ square

(E) Two pink 2 ⁷/₈″ squares cut in half once on the diagonal

BLOCK PIECING INSTRUCTIONS:
This block is constructed as a nine-patch that has two narrow rows and one wider row in the center.

A. First sew four pink triangles to the center 3 ³/₈″ square.

B. Next sew the four units that consist of a brown triangle and two blue triangles.

C. Sew two of the brown triangle segments to the center block to form the center row.

D. Sew two pink squares to the ends of two of the brown triangle segments.

E. Sew these two rows to the center row as seen in the diagram above. When piecing the triangles together, press the seams out towards the smaller triangles.

F. On the top and bottom row press the seams from the center out towards each side.

G. On the middle row press the seams from the out side in towards the center of the block.

Fun Fleece Scarf

The block acts as a sleeve to insert the other end of the scarf through.

Needle Book

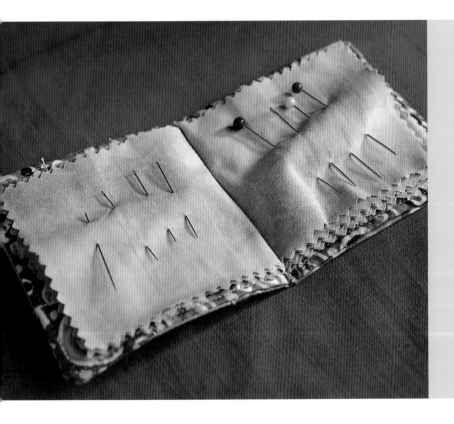

$\mathcal{S}$ ewers need needles all the time, and tend to keep them in a pincushion where they are hard to find amongst the pins and sometimes disappear down into the cushion. This is a really easy-to-make, little cloth book for storing all your different needles so you easily find the ones you want to use. You can even label each page with a fabric pen to help in organizing different types and sizes of needles.

Needle Book

MATERIALS:

Note: Read through these instructions thoroughly before cutting any fabric so that you will understand the process to use for figuring the sizes of fabric and batting you need.

- One 3 $^1/_2$″ - 6 $^1/_2$″ ($^1/_2$″ smaller finished) **quilt block**
- One piece of coordinating fabric the same size as the block you choose to use
- One piece of batting at least 6 $^1/_2$″ x 12 $^1/_2$″ (you need your piece of batting the same size as the block and square sewn together)
- Several large scraps of fabric for the book pages (batiks work best for these pages)

INSTRUCTIONS:

Top cover with pieced block

A. Cut one piece of coordinating fabric the same size as the quilt block you choose.

B. Place the pieced block and the same size square of fabric right-sides together and sew a $^1/_4$″ seam down one side. *(Note: If the quilt block is directional, then you will want to sew the seam on the right hand side of the pieces).*

Back cover of coordinating fabric and quilted

D. Cut a second piece of coordinating fabric and batting the same size as the piece ends up above. (This project uses a piece 3 $^1/_2$″ x 6 $^1/_2$″).

E. Layer the batting, backing face-up and the top (block) piece face-down and sew the three layers together leaving a 2″ (or larger) opening in one side.

F. Turn right-side out and hand-stitch up the opening closed.

G. Quilt this piece in any manner you choose.

Cut pages to hold needles and assemble

Cut 4 - 6 pieces about one inch smaller in size on all sides out of scraps and cut with pinking shears or a pinking blade on your rotary cutter for pages.

Assemble and stitch the Needle Book

Stack the fabric pages together neatly on the inside of the top of the quilted book cover making sure to center them on the cover and topstitch down the middle of the pages so that the pages are now attached to the book. The stitching will help the book fold in the center.

NINE-PATCH BLOCK

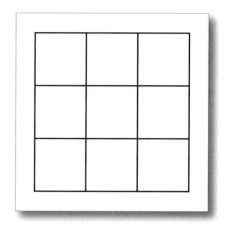

3″ FINISHED BLOCK
(A) Five green 1 $^1/_2$″ squares ☐
(B) Four yellow 1 $^1/_2$″ squares ☐

BLOCK PIECING INSTRUCTIONS:

A. Sew the squares together alternating the colors like a tic-tac-toe board, pressing the seams of the top and bottom rows one way and the middle row the opposite way.

3″ FINISHED BLOCK

(A) **Four purple 1 ¼″ squares**

(B) **Two purple 2 ¾″ squares cut in half twice on the diagonal**

(C) **Four orange 1 ⅝″ squares cut in half once on the diagonal**

(D) **One purple print 2″ square**

BLOCK PIECING INSTRUCTIONS:

This block is constructed as a nine-patch that has two narrow rows and one wider row in the center.

B. First sew the four units that consist of a brown dot triangle and two cream triangles.

C. Sew two of the brown triangle segments to the center block to form the center row.

D. Sew two brown dot squares to the ends of two of the brown dot triangle segments.

E. Sew these two rows to the center row as seen in the diagram above. When piecing the triangles together, press the seams out towards the smaller triangles.

F. On the top and bottom row press the seams from the center out towards each side.

G. On the middle row press the seams from the outside in towards the center of the block.

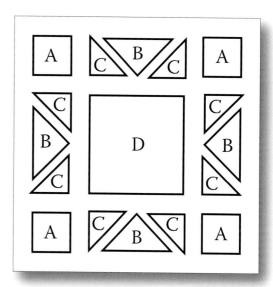

CD and DVD Book

Do you have CD cases scattered everywhere? How about broken CD cases with the CDs lying around? This project is a really easy answer to the problems associated with CDs. You can make a different cloth CD book for different music or movie genres and make several for all of your friends and family.

MATERIALS:

Note: Read through these instructions thoroughly before cutting any fabric so that you will understand the process used for figuring the sizes of fabric and batting you need.

- **One 6 $\frac{1}{2}$" - 8 $\frac{1}{2}$" ($\frac{1}{2}$" smaller finished) quilt block**
- **One piece of coordinatingfabric the same size as the block you choose to use**
- **One piece of coordinating fabric at least 8 $\frac{1}{2}$" x 17" square (depends on size of block used)**
- **One piece of batting at least 8 $\frac{1}{2}$" x 17"**
- **Several fat quarters or $\frac{1}{2}$ yard of fabric for the book pages (batiks work best for these pages because they tend to fray less than other fabrics and they are nice looking on both sides)**

INSTRUCTIONS:

A. Cut a piece of coordinating fabric the same size as your quilt block.

B. Place the pieced block and the same size square of fabric together facing each other and sew a $\frac{1}{4}$" seam down one side (if the quilt block is directional, then you will want to sew the seam on the right hand side of the pieces.

C. Cut a second piece of coordinating fabric and a piece of batting the same size as this newly sewn piece (this project uses a piece 8 $\frac{1}{2}$" x 16 $\frac{1}{2}$").

D. Layer the batting, backing face-up and the top piece face-down together and sew together leaving a 2" (or larger) hole in one side. Turn right-side out and hand-stitch up the hole.

E. Quilt this piece in any manner you choose.

F. Cut 4 - 6 pieces twice the height of the cover and about an inch smaller in the width out of the coordinating fabric with pinking shears or using a pinking blade on your rotary cutter for pages (13" x 15 $\frac{1}{2}$" pieces were used in this project).

G. Lay out each 13" x 15 $\frac{1}{2}$" piece with a 15 $\frac{1}{2}$" side facing you and fold the bottom up to about 1 $\frac{1}{2}$"

below the top. Sew up the edges using a top-stitch with a coordinating thread about a $\frac{1}{2}$" from the edge.

H. Stack the fabric pages together neatly on the inside of the top of the quilted book cover making sure to center them on the cover and topstitch down the middle of the pages so that the pages are now attached to the book. The stitches will help the book fold in the center.

SAW-TOOTH STAR BLOCK

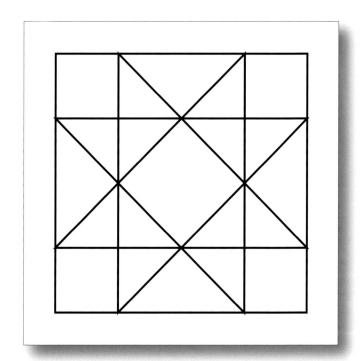

C. Sew two of the brown triangle segments to the center block to form the center row.

D. Sew two brown dot squares to the ends of two of the brown dot triangle segments.

E. Sew these two rows to the center row as seen in the diagram above. When piecing the triangles together, press the seams out towards the smaller triangles.

F. On the top and bottom row press the seams from the center out towards each side.

G. On the middle row press the seams from the outside in towards the center of the block.

8″ FINISHED BLOCK

(A) **Four brown dot 2 $\frac{1}{2}$″ squares**

(B) **One brown dot 5 $\frac{1}{2}$″ square cut in half twice on the diagonal**

(C) **Four cream 2 $\frac{7}{8}$″ squares cut in half once on the diagonal**

(D) **One brown print 3 $\frac{3}{8}$″ square**

(E) **Two black 2 $\frac{7}{8}$″ squares cut in half once on the diagonal**

BLOCK PIECING INSTRUCTIONS:

This block is constructed as a nine-patch that has two narrow rows and one wider row in the center.

A. First sew four black triangles to the center 3 $\frac{3}{8}$″ square.

B. Next sew the four units that consist of a brown dot triangle and two cream triangles.

Teacher's Tote

*T*his is a great gift for your favorite teacher or even a bus driver. Make it with your favorite fun fabric and you'll find hundreds of things you need to tote around.

MATERIALS:

- **One 12 $\frac{1}{2}$″ (12″ finished) quilt block (a windmill block was used for this project)**
- **$\frac{3}{4}$ yard of coordinating fabric for outside of bag**
- **$\frac{3}{4}$ yard of coordinating fabric for lining (can be same as outside)**
- **One 20″ x 41″ piece of batting**
- **Two 41″ pieces of 1″ wide belting (in a coordinating color if you choose not to cover)**
- **Optional-Two 41″ x 3″ pieces of coordinating fabric to cover the belting**
- **$\frac{1}{2}$ yard of the same fabric as the outside of the bag for bias binding**

INSTRUCTIONS:

A. Cut two 2 $\frac{1}{2}$″ x 12 $\frac{1}{2}$″ strips, one 3″ x 16 $\frac{1}{2}$″ strip and one 4 $\frac{1}{2}$″ x 16 $\frac{1}{2}$″ strip from the fabric you will use on the outside of the bag.

B. Cut one 23″ x 19″ piece from the fabric you will use on the outside of the bag.

C. Sew the 12 $\frac{1}{2}$″ strips to the sides of the block.

D. Sew the 3″ x 16 $\frac{1}{2}$″ strip to the top of the block and the 4 $\frac{1}{2}$″ x 16 $\frac{1}{2}$″ strip to the bottom of the block.

E. Sew the 23″ x 19″ piece of fabric to one side of the bordered block making one big piece approximately 19″ x 39″.

F. Cut a 20″ x 40″ piece from the backing fabric.

G. Layer the backing, batting, and top piece for quilting and quilt in any manner you choose.

H. Make 1 $\frac{1}{2}$ yards of bias binding. Use leftovers from a previous project or buy ready-made bias binding (see general instructions for making bias binding).

I. Sew the binding on the top outside edge of the bag and fold over to the inside to hand-sew.

J. Wrap each piece of belting with the 3″ x 41″ strips of fabric making sure to fold in the raw edges and then topstitch down the length of the straps on both edges of the strap.

K. Pin the ends of one strap to the inside of the front of the bag about 4″ in from the sides and about 2″ down into the bag. Pin the other strap in the same manner to the back side of the bag.

L. Topstitch the straps on with a coordinating thread in an "x" pattern right below the edge of the binding for reinforcement.

VARIATION OF PINWHEEL BLOCK

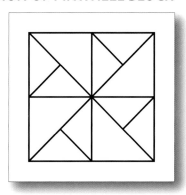

12″ FINISHED BLOCK

(A) One blue 6 $\frac{7}{8}$″ square cut in half on the diagonal

(B) One yellow 6 $\frac{7}{8}$″ square cut in half on the diagonal

(C) One pink 6 $\frac{7}{8}$″ square cut in half on the diagonal

(D) One green 6 $\frac{7}{8}$″ square cut in half on the diagonal

Note: The triangles in steps A-D can also be made all the same, in which case you would need two 6 $\frac{7}{8}$″ squares of the same color cut in half on the diagonal.

(E) Two blue print 7 $\frac{1}{4}$″ squares cut twice on the diagonal

(F) Two 7 $\frac{1}{4}$″ squares cut twice on the diagonal, the same fabric you are using for the rest of the bag. A black print with crayons on it was used here

BLOCK PIECING INSTRUCTIONS:

A. Sew a blue triangle to a black print triangle to make the larger sized triangles that you see in the other half of each unit.

B. Sew the pieced triangles to the larger triangles.

FOR BABY

*L*ittle bundles of joy deserve handmade gifts from the heart. Whether it's a soft fleece play toy with stimulating colors or a very useful burp rag, your little one will love these easy-to-make treasures.

Burp Cloth

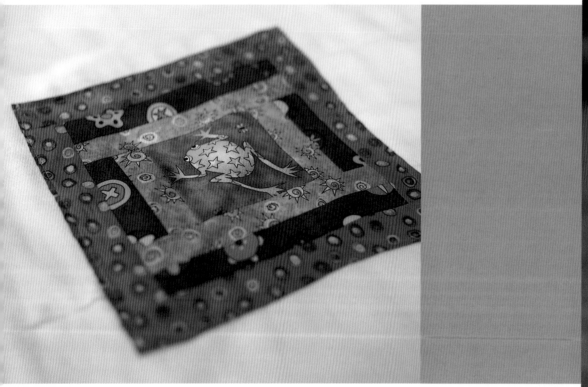

𝒫arents with infants just can't live without burp
cloths and if we have to have them, they might as
well be cute. Here is an easy way to spice up some cloth
diapers for a really fun, but handy burp cloth for your
baby. Or, make a set of three as a great new baby gift!

Burp Cloth

MATERIALS:

- One 6 $^1/_2$″ - 10 $^1/_2$″ ($^1/_2$″ smaller finished) quilt block: (an 8 $^1/_2$″, 8″ finished, block was used for this project)
- Two 3″ x 15″ strips of fabric that coordinates with the quilt block
- One cloth diaper

INSTRUCTIONS:

Stitch the block to the diaper

A. Fold a $^1/_4$″ hem around the block and sew to the center of one side of the cloth diaper using a top-stitch or blind-hem stitch.

Make the trim for the long ends of the diaper

B. Fold the ends of the strips in about $^1/_2$″.

C. Fold each side into the middle so that the raw edges on the long ends meat each other in the middle of each strip.

D. Fold the strip in half the long-way and press so all raw edges are covered.

Finish by topstitching the trim

E. Pin one strip to each end of the diaper so that the ends of the diaper are covered and topstitch right at the edge of the strip.

Make these in sets of threes for new baby gifts and perhaps use holiday themed blocks and coordinating fabric for the trim as a gift to parents with a new infant over a holiday period.

VARIATION ON LOG CABIN BLOCK

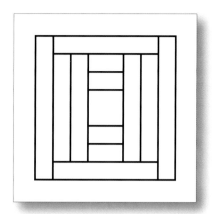

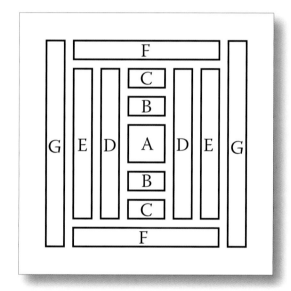

9″ FINISHED BLOCK

(A) One 3 $^1/_2$″ square of focus fabric
(B) Two yellow 1 $^1/_2$″ x 3 $^1/_2$″ rectangles
(C) Two purple print 1 $^1/_2$″ x 3 $^1/_2$″ rectangles
(D) Two yellow 1 $^1/_2$″ x 7 $^1/_2$″ rectangles
(E) Two purple print 1 $^1/_2$″ x 7 $^1/_2$″ rectangles
(F) Two orange print 1 $^1/_2$″ x 7 $^1/_2$″ rectangles
(G) Two orange print 1 $^1/_2$″ x 9 $^1/_2$″ rectangles

BLOCK PIECING INSTRUCTIONS:

A. Start with the small square and add the rectangle of the same size to one side.

B. Going in a counter-clockwise direction sew each set of next sized larger strips to the block as seen in the diagram above.

Cuddly Toy

This is a great small cuddly blanket to take along in the stroller or baby-seat to entertain that special little one. The bright blocks and fringed edges are sure to catch their attention.

Cuddly Toy

MATERIALS:
- Two 9 ½" - 12 ½" (½" smaller finished) quilt blocks (can be the same block or two different ones)
- Two 16" squares of polar fleece (two different colors are nice)
- Two 3" x 32" strips of polar fleece (two different colors are nice)

INSTRUCTIONS:
A. Fold a ¼" hem around the blocks and sew one quilt block to the center of each piece of polar fleece using a top-stitch or a blind-hem stitch.
B. Cut the strips along one side every ½" and about 2 ½" deep so that you make fringe all along one side of both strips.
C. Lay one 16" square face-up and pin the two strips to it so that the fringe is pointing into the middle of the square.
D. Lay the second 16" square face-down on top of the first square.
E. Starting on one side, sew all around the squares with a ¼" seam, stopping 3" from where you started.
F. Turn the project right-side out and sew the hole up with a blind-hem stitch.

VARIATION DIAMOND IN A SQUARE

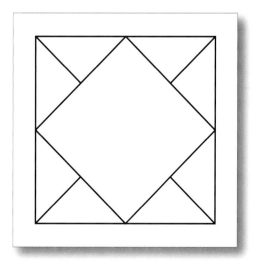

10" FINISHED BLOCK
(A) One 7 ⅝" square of focus fabric ☐
(B) One orange print 6 ¼" rectangle cut in half twice on the diagonal ⊠
(C) One purple print 6 ¼" rectangle cut in half twice on the diagonal ⊠

BLOCK PIECING INSTRUCTIONS:
A. Sew four pairs of small triangles together to make the larger triangles seen in the photograph.
B Sew one large triangle to each side of the focus fabric square.

Fuzzy Blanket

*B*abies use many blankets throughout their childhood. This is a super easy blanket you can make for all the babies in your life. It holds up well to wear and tear, is very warm and is great to use in the stroller on gloomy days to keep the rain away.

Fuzzy Baby Blanket

MATERIALS:

- One piece of polyester fleece about 40″ square
- A couple of 8 ¹/₂″ - 10 ¹/₂″ (¹/₂″ smaller finished) pieced blocks (three were used in this project)
- Thread for topstitching blocks onto blanket (the blocks can be hand-stitched on if you choose)

INSTRUCTIONS:

A. Make 2″- 3″ deep cuts 1″ apart all along the outside edge of the 40″ square of fleece.

B. Fold a ¹/₄″ seam on all the edges of the pieced blocks.

C. Press a ¹/₂″ seam around the edge of the blocks, pin the blocks to the fleece and topstitch or hand-stitch them on using the blind-hem stitch.

VARIATION ON LOG CABIN BLOCK

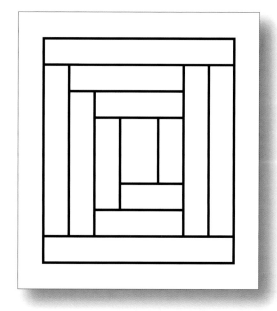

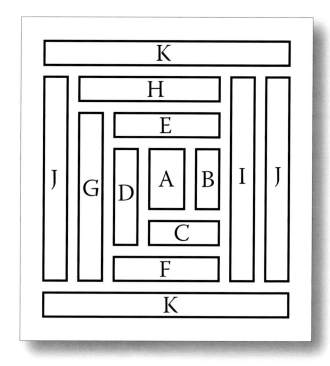

9″ FINISHED BLOCK

(A) One green 3 ¹/₂″ x 4 ¹/₂″ square of focus fabric
(B) One green 1 ¹/₄″ x 4 ¹/₂″ rectangle
(C) One green 1 ¹/₄″ x 3 ²/₄″ rectangle
(D) One dark green 1 ¹/₄″ x 5″ rectangle
(E) One dark green 1 ¹/₄″ x 4 ¹/₂″ rectangle
(F) One blue 1 ¹/₄″ x 4 ¹/₂″ rectangle
(G) One blue 1 ³/₄″ x 6 ¹/₂″ rectangle
(H) One blue 1 ¹/₄″ x 6 rectangle
(I) One blue 1 ³/₄″ x 7 ¹/₄″ rectangle
(J) Two purple 1 ³/₄″ x 8 ¹/₄″ rectangles
(K) Two purple 1 ³/₄″ x 9 ¹/₄″ rectangles

BLOCK PIECING INSTRUCTIONS:

A. Start with the small square and add the rectangle of the same size to one side.

B. Then sew strips on according to the letters in the diagram

VARIATION OF PUSS IN THE CORNER BLOCK
*Used for two of the three blocks

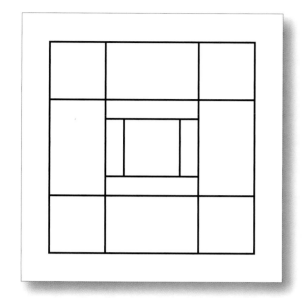

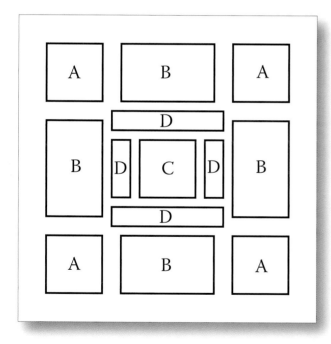

BLOCK PIECING INSTRUCTIONS:

A. Sew two strips to the side of the 3″ square and then a strip to the top and the bottom of the square.

B. Sew a rectangle to each side of the pieced center block.

C. Sew two 2 ½″ squares to the ends of two of the rectangles.

D. Sew the three rows together as seen in the diagram above.

8″ FINISHED BLOCK (SEW 2 OF THESE)
(A) Four purple stripe 2 ½″ squares
(B) Four green print 2 ½″ x 4 ½″ rectangles
(C) One novelty print 3″ square
(D) Four blue print 1 ½″ x 4 ½″ strips

GIFTS AND ACCESSORIES

$\mathcal{W}$e live in a time when almost nothing is hand-made. In these times you know a gift is very special if the giver took the time to sit and make it. These are the gifts that are most cherished.

Travel Pillow

$\mathcal{A}$ pillow always comes in handy on long car trips. This adorable little pillow will make your travels a bit more comfortable. It has a handy pocket for a book, hanky, or maybe a favorite stuffed animal.

GIFTS AND ACCESSORIES

Travel Pillow

MATERIALS:

- One 9 $\frac{1}{2}$″ (9″ finished) quilt block (a churn dash block was used in this project)
- One 9 $\frac{1}{2}$″ piece of batting
- One 9 $\frac{1}{2}$″ piece of backing fabric
- One pillow form at least 14″ square, but 14″ x 20″ works well
- Two pieces of fabric for pillow case that are larger than the pillow form by three inches at one end and by one inch at the other end; (for example 15″ x 23″ pieces were used for this project for a pillow form that was 14″ x 20″)
- Five coordinating buttons (depending on the size of the pillow and the size of the buttons, you may need more or perhaps even fewer buttons)

INSTRUCTIONS:

Assemble Quilt Block

A. Layer and sew together the 9 $\frac{1}{2}$″ block with the batting first, the backing fabric face-up next and the pieced block face-down last.

B. Stitch these together beginning to sew in the middle of one side and sew around the outer edge of your block leaving a 3″ opening hole on the side you started on.

C. Trim the edges and corners neatly. Turn your block right side out and poke out the corners so they are crisply pointed. Fold in the fabric and batting at the opening with the same seam allowances and iron in preparation for sewing the opening closed. Set aside for the next step.

Attach pocket to the front piece of pillow case

D. Pin the block onto the middle of one side (the front) of the pillow cover and topstitch down one side, across the bottom and up the other side, leaving the top open to be a pocket.

Pillow Case

E. Pin the two 15″ x 23″ pieces of fabric together right-sides together and sew a $\frac{1}{2}$″ seam on three sides of the pillow case leaving the fourth open (on a rectangular pillow, leave one shorter side open).

F. Turn the pillow right side out and press.

G. Fold the open front side of the pillow case down inside the pillow about 1 $\frac{1}{2}$″ and pin. Sew approximately five button holes into this band of the pillow case evenly interspersed (if you prefer the buttons not to be seen on the front side of the pillow, then you will sew the fold and the button holes on the back side of the pillow).

Finishing

H. Sew buttons on the right side of the other side of the pillow case where they will line up with the button holes.

I. The button side of the case should fold over the end of the pillow and under the side with the buttonholes bringing the buttons to the top of the opposite side when they are buttoned, keeping the pillow case securely in place as it gets moved around the car, carried to and from the car, the plane, the hotel.

Travel Pillow

CHURN DASH BLOCK

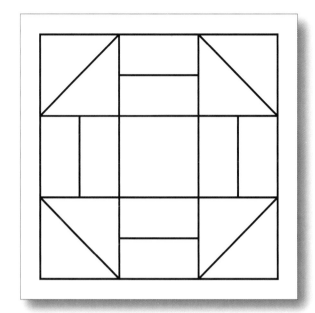

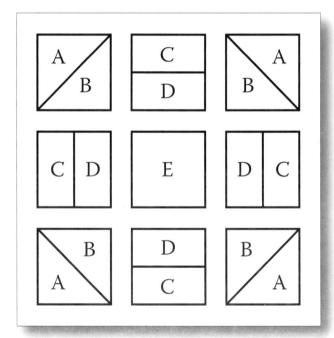

9″ FINISHED BLOCK

(A) Two 3 ⁷/₈″ yellow squares cut in half on the diagonal

(B) Two 3 ⁷/₈″ green squares cut in half on the diagonal

(C) Four 3 ¹/₂″ x 2 ¹/₂″ yellow rectangles

(D) Four 3 ¹/₂″ x 2 ¹/₂″ green rectangles

(E) One 3 ¹/₂″ cream print square

BLOCK PIECING INSTRUCTIONS:

A. Sew the pairs of triangles and the pairs rectangles together as seen in the diagram. Press the seams here towards the darker fabric.

B. Piece the sewn blocks into three rows and then the rows into a nine-patch to get the finished block.

C. When piecing the blocks into their rows, press the top and bottom rows' seams towards the center and the middle rows' seams towards the outside.

D. When piecing the rows together, press the row seams towards the center row.

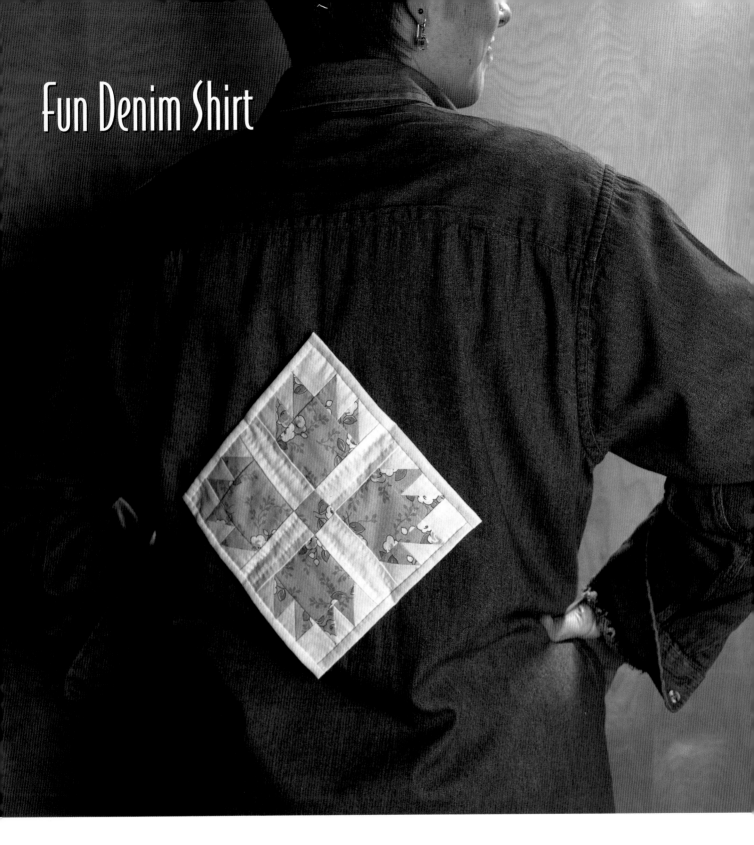

Fun Denim Shirt

$\mathcal{I}$f you love quilting, add it to your clothing so you can show off your abilities and jazz up your attire. This is a really easy way to personalize an over-shirt. The blocks can be easily replaced so you can refresh your wardrobe if you choose.

GIFTS AND ACCESSORIES

Fun Denim Shirt

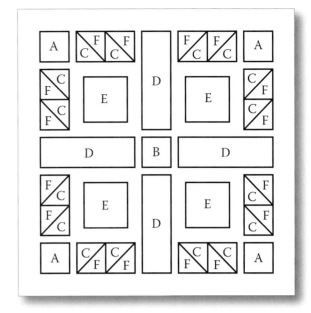

MATERIALS:

- One store-bought denim shirt
- One 6 $\frac{1}{2}$" -10 $\frac{1}{2}$" ($\frac{1}{2}$" smaller finished) quilt block
- Four 1" x 10" strips to bind the block
- One piece of batting the same size as the block

INSTRUCTIONS:

A. Cut four 1" strips for each block (cut the strips a little longer than the length of the block).

B. Sew a strip to each side of the block and then one to the top and bottom of the block.

C. Center the batting on the back of the block and quilt in the ditch around the piecing in the block.

D. Fold the strips around to the back like binding and baste in place to the batting.

E. Hand-stitch the block to the back of the shirt using a blind-hem stitch, making sure to center the block on the back of the shirt.

BEARS PAW BLOCK - VARIATION

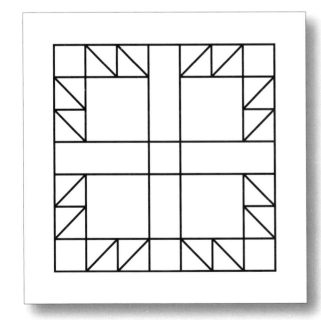

8" FINISHED BLOCK

(A) **Four cream 1 $\frac{5}{8}$" squares**

(B) **One blue print 1 $\frac{5}{8}$" square**

(C) **Eight blue print 2" squares cut in half on the diagonal**

(D) **Four cream 1 $\frac{5}{8}$" x 3 $\frac{7}{8}$" rectangles**

(E) **Four blue print 2 $\frac{3}{4}$" squares**

(F) **Eight cream 2" squares cut in half on the diagonal**

BLOCK PIECING INSTRUCTIONS:

A. Sew the 1 $\frac{5}{8}$" center square to two of the cream colored rectangles.

B. Sew pairs of cream and blue triangles together to make squares.

C. Sew the half-square triangle units together into eight sets of two.

D. Sew four of the pairs to a cream square so that you have four rows of three blocks and four rows of two blocks.

E. Sew the rows of two blocks to the 2 $\frac{3}{4}$" squares and then sew the three block rows to one side as seen in the diagram.

F. Sew two pairs of paws together with a cream rectangle in between and then sew the three rows together.

G. Press all your seams towards the blue fabric.

Christmas Ornaments

I like to give a new ornament to all the children in my life every year. By the time they are grown they should have a nice collection to start their own traditions with when they are on their own. Ornaments are a quick, easy quilting project that you can make for your own tree or as a gift for others. This project can also be made into easy coasters by omitting the ribbon step. This is a good way to introduce kids to quilting because it is a small manageable project.

Christmas Ornaments

MATERIALS:
- **One 6″ quilt block**
- **One 6 ¹/₂″ piece of backing fabric**
- **One 6 ¹/₂″ piece of batting**
- **Pieces of thin ribbon at least 8″ long in coordinating colors (if you are making coasters you do not need any ribbon)**

INSTRUCTIONS:

You can make these ornaments with any quilt block you choose. These were made with a nine-patch.

A. Put together your 6 ¹/₂″ block with the batting first, the backing face-up next and the pieced block face-down last.

B. Pin both ends of a piece of ribbon into one corner of the block between the backing and the top, making sure the loop of ribbon is tucked in between the layers, and that the loop does not get caught in the stitches.

C. Starting in the middle of one side, sew around the outer edge of your block leaving a 3″ opening on the side you started. Trim the edges and corners neatly. Turn your block right-side out and poke out the corners. Fold in the fabric and batting at the opening and iron in preparation for sewing shut.

D. Hand-stitch the opening shut.

E. Hand-quilt the block around the piecing.

An option for this block is to cut the four corners on a 45° angle before finishing. This will create a finished block in an octagon shape.

Another option if making coasters is to add a heat resistant batting to the coasters to make them reflect back the temperature of the beverage toward the cup and away from the furniture.

NINE-PATCH

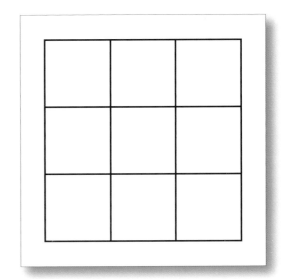

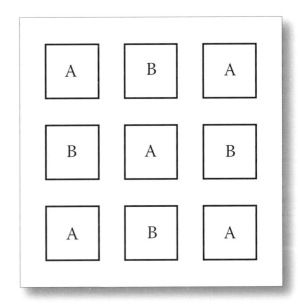

6″ FINISHED BLOCK
- **Nine 2 ¹/₂″ squares (five red, four copper)**

BLOCK PIECING INSTRUCTIONS:

A. Sew the squares together alternating the colors like a tic-tac-toe board, pressing the seams of the top and bottom rows one way and the middle row the opposite way.

Holiday Centerpiece

This is a useful, but pretty tool for getting casseroles from the oven to the table without awkward fumbling of oven mitts. It doubles as a nice table runner, as well.

MATERIALS:

- One 12 ¹/₂″ (12″ finished) quilt block (a log cabin block was used in this project)
- Two 12 ¹/₂″ squares of complementary fabric for outer squares
- Six 12 ¹/₂″ squares of cotton batting
- Three 12 ¹/₂″ squares of heat resistant batting
- Three 12 ¹/₂″ squares of complementary fabric for backing

INSTRUCTIONS

A. Put together your 12 ¹/₂″ blocks with the batting first, the backing face-up next and the pieced block face-down last. Starting in the middle of one side of each block, sew around the outer edges of your blocks leaving a 5″ opening on the side you started. Trim the edges and corners neatly. Turn your blocks right-side out and poke out the corners. Sew up the hole using a blind-hem stitch. Set aside for the next step.

B. At this point you can quilt each block in any manner you choose or leave unquilted. The blocks used in this project were topstitched with a decorative leaf stitch about ¹/₂″ inside the outer edge of each block.

C. Lay the pieced block with one corner overlapping a corner of one of the other two quilted squares on one side and overlapping the other square on the other side as seen in diagram E.

D. Hand-sew the blocks together using a blind-hem stitch on the top and the bottom of the overlapping corners.

E.

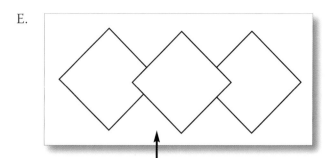

Pieced Block

Hand-sew the blocks to each other where they overlap on the top and the bottom using a blind-hem stitch.

LOG CABIN BLOCK

Holiday Centerpiece

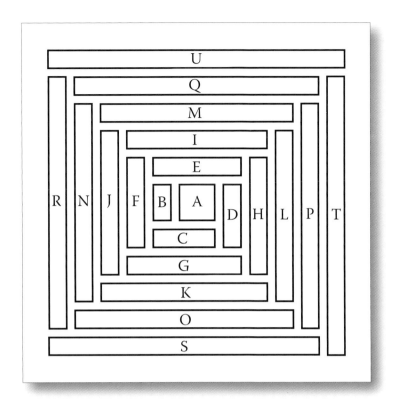

11″ FINISHED BLOCK

(A) One 1 ¹/₂″ green print square of focus fabric

(B) One 1 ¹/₂″ gold print rectangle

(C) One 1 ¹/₂″ x 2 ¹/₂″ gold rectangle

(D) One 1 ¹/₂″ x 3 ¹/₂″ red print rectangle

(E) One 1 ¹/₂″ x 2 ¹/₂″ green print rectangle

(F) One 1 ¹/₂″ x 3 ¹/₂″ gold print rectangle

(G) One 1 ¹/₂″ x 4 ¹/₂″ gold print rectangle

(H) One 1 ¹/₂″ x 4 ¹/₂″ green print rectangle

(I) One 1 ¹/₂″ x 5 ¹/₂″ red print rectangle

(J) One 1 ¹/₂″ x 5 ¹/₂″ gold print rectangle

(K) One 1 ¹/₂″ x 6 ¹/₂″ gold rectangle

(L) One 1 ¹/₂″ x 6 ¹/₂″ red print rectangle

(M) One 1 ¹/₂″ x 7 ¹/₂″ green print rectangle

(N) One 1 ¹/₂″ x 7 ¹/₂″ gold rectangle

(O) One 1 ¹/₂″ x 8 ¹/₂″ gold print rectangle

(P) One 1 ¹/₂″ x 8 ¹/₂″ green print rectangle

(Q) One 1 ¹/₂″ x 9 ¹/₂″ red print rectangle

(R) One 1 ¹/₂″ x 7 ¹/₂″ gold print rectangle

(S) One 1 ¹/₂″ x 10 ¹/₂″ gold print rectangle

(T) One 1 ¹/₂″ x 10 ¹/₂″ red print rectangle

(U) One 1 ¹/₂″ x 11 ¹/₂″ green print rectangle

BLOCK PIECING INSTRUCTIONS:

A. Start with the small square and add the rectangle of the same size to one side.

B. Going in a counter-clockwise direction, sew each set of next sized larger strips to the block as seen in the diagram.

Christmas Table Topper

$\mathscr{Y}$ou can make a beautiful table topper very quickly and easily using a 20″ quilt block, adding a border, quilting it and binding it. By adding a layer of insulating material you can make a practical and pretty hot pad for holiday entertaining.

Christmas Table Topper

MATERIALS:

- One 20 $^1/_2$″ (20″ finished) square quilt block
- Four 4″ x 29″ strips of coordinating fabric
- One 28″ square piece of flannel for batting
  A variation of this can be used as a festive and decorative hot pad *
- One 28″ square piece of coordinating fabric for backing
- $^1/_2$ yard piece of coordinating fabric for binding
- Machine thread in a coordinating color to quilt your piece

INSTRUCTIONS:

Quilt the Block

A. Border the for the 20 $^1/_2$″ pieced quilt block with the four 4″ strips.

B. Square up the top.

C. Layer the backing fabric face up, the batting and the bordered top face up and quilt in any manner you choose.

Finish by making the binding and bind the top

D. Make 3 $^1/_2$ yards of bias binding, use leftovers from a previous project or buy ready-made bias binding (see general instructions for making bias binding).

E. Machine-sew binding onto front of quilted topper.

F. Wrap binding over edge of topper and hand sew binding to the back topper.

*Festive hot pad variation

G. At step C layer the back, one piece of cotton batting, a piece of heat resistant batting, another piece of cotton batting and the quilt block with its stitched borders and quilt in any manner you choose.

VARIATION SAW TOOTH STAR BLOCK
20″ FINISHED BLOCK

(A) Two 7 $^1/_4$″ squares of cream print cut in half twice on the diagonal ⊠

(B) One 6 $^1/_2$″ square of cream print □

(C) Eight 3 $^1/_2$″ squares of cream print □

(D) Two 4 $^1/_4$″ squares of cream print cut in half twice on the diagonal ⊠

(E) One 7 $^1/_4$″ square of a green print cut in half twice on the diagonal ⊠

(F) Eight 3 $^7/_8$″ squares of a green print cut in half once on the diagonal ◹

(G) Four 2 $^5/_8$″ red squares □

BLOCK PIECING INSTRUCTIONS:

A. Sew four sets of one red square to two small cream triangles as seen in the picture. Sew a triangle cut from the 3 $^7/_8$″ green print squares to each end of these four sets.

B. Sew a cream 3 $^1/_2$″ square to each end of two of these sets.

C. Sew the two without the end squares to the cream 6 $^1/_4$″ square.

D. Sew the two remaining sets to the other sides of the larger square and set this block aside for later.

E. Sew four sets of cream triangles cut from the 7 $^1/_4$″ cream square to the two short sides of a green triangle cut from the 7 $^1/_4$″ green square.

F. Sew a long side of the green triangle cut from the green 3 $^7/_8$″ squares to each end of the units pieced in step E.

G. Sew a unit pieced in step F to two opposite sides of the block set aside earlier in step D.

H. Sew a cream 3 $^1/_2$″ square to each end of the two remaining units from step F.

I. Sew the two rows from step H to the two remaining sides of the block.

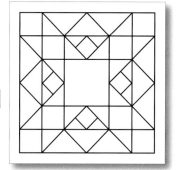

About the Designers

ARLENE PORETSKY

Arlene was taught to sew by her aunt when she was a young child, first by hand and then on a treadle sewing machine, which she still has today. She decided to make her own quilt for an antique bed. From that day forward, quilting has become a passionate form of art expression for Arlene. She loves picking fabrics and modifying and creating patterns.

CAROL JAYNES

Carol purchased a long-arm quilting machine and has created a booming business dealing with the most honest and fun group of people she's ever been involved with. Carol is a 35 year Georgia resident with two grown children and too many cats.

ELTANGIER TRAMMELL

Eltangier got her first sewing machine when she was 12 years old and she has been sewing ever since, mostly in home decorating. She discovered quilting when she became an employee at Intown Quilters in 2004 and lives in Atlanta with her two sons, Bryant and Chad and their dogs, Buddy and Sky.

SHEILA BLAIR

After sewing most of her life, Sheila Blair took up quilting in 1990 and has been doing it ever since. She loves playing with 100% cotton fabrics, especially working with the customers at Intown Quilters in Atlanta, and "...the challenge of mixing colors...making them pop and sing!"

SHANNON BAKER

Shannon grew up in the mountains of Tennessee where she was inspired to quilt at a young age. She is working towards designing patterns and fabric of her own, and loves creating her own art-quilts. Shannon lives in Atlanta and works at The Red Hen quilt shop in Marietta, GA.

PATTY MURPHY

Patty is an accomplished quilter. She began sewing as a child and found her passion for quilting as a teenager. Later, after requests for quilts from friends and family, she began quilting professionally. Patty lives with her husband, Michael, and dog, Lady, in Atlanta, Georgia, where she also works part-time at Intown Quilters.

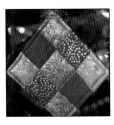

JOAN WIEZENTHAL

Joan grew up in Florida and moved to Atlanta in 1971. She took up quilting in 2003 after a lifetime of sewing. Joan is the manager of Intown Quilters quilt shop in Atlanta, GA.

Quilting Terminolgy

¼ INCH SEAM

The size seam most often called for in piecing for the purpose of quilting. Many quilters feel this is the most important thing to be able to do for quilting.

APPLIQUÉ

A method of hand-stitching to sew pieces of fabric on top of other pieces of fabric.

BACKING

The material that you put on the back of a quilt.

BASTE

Temporarily stitching the three layers of a quilt together to hold the layers in place while the quilting is done. Basting can be done with thread, safety pins or spray-baste.

BATTING

A sheet of cotton, cotton-poly blend, wool or silk filling used in the middle of quilts to add thickness, warmth, and dimension to the layers of fabric.

BIAS

A diagonal cut or fold in cloth. The bias cut will have more stretch than a cross or straignt grain cut. The bias cut is useful for bindings, but can cause some difficulty in piecing.

BINDING

The outside finishing edge that is put on the outside of a quilt. It covers the raw edges formed by the backing, batting and top. It should be doubled and may be cut from the crosswise grain of the fabric for straight edged quilts. Curved edge quilts require bias binding.

BLIND-HEM STITCH

A stitch that goes in one side of a seam exactly opposite where it came out the other side of the seam so that the stitches lock together making them fairly invisible.

BLOCK

Usually several pieces of fabric sewn together in a pattern to form a larger square.

CORNER STONES

Squares the same size as a border or sashing that go in between the corners of blocks or at the outside corners of a quilt.

CUTTING MAT

A self-healing cutting surface that is used with a rotary cutter blade and a ruler to cut fabric for sewing and sometimes paper for crafts.

FACE-UP/DOWN

When layering a top with batting and backing the nice side of the top or back is considered the face and it will be put face-up or face-down at different stages of sewing.

MITERING

The joining of two perpendicular border strips using a 45° angle. The effect is somewhat like a picture frame.

PIECE

A word that is used to call the process of sewing together pieces of fabric in quilting.

PRESS

Using an iron to flatten seams and fabric by pressing straight down on the fabric as opposed to pushing the iron back and forth across the fabric. This causes less distortion of the fabric.

QUILTING

Stitches used to hold a back, batting, and a top together-- making a quilt. This can be done by hand or machine.

Quilting Terminolgy

QUILT TOP
A group of pieced blocks sewn together, usually with one or more borders that will be a top of a finished quilt.

RIGHT-SIDES TOGETHER
Putting the nice sides of two pieces of fabric towards each other for piecing.

ROTARY CUTTER
A cutting tool that uses a round blade for continuous cutting. It is very similar to a pizza cutter and is usually used with a straight edge.

ROTARY CUTTING RULERS
Rulers that are usually made out of clear acrylic and marked extensively with measurements on all four sides of the ruler. These rulers come in all different shapes and sizes.

RUNNING STITCH
A Stitch that goes down into and back up through layers of fabric over and over.

SANDWICH
The layers of a piece of fabric face-down, a piece of batting next, and then a piece of fabric face-up on top in preparation for quilting.

SASHING
The fabric strips that go in between the blocks in a quilt. Usually it is used with corner stones.

SCANT SEAM
A seam that is a tiny bit smaller than the seam that is called for. Some patterns call for a scant seam so that the pieces fit together well.

SELVEDGE/SELVAGE
The edge of a fabric that is woven so that it will not fray or ravel. Most fabric has a selvedge on two sides.

STRIP-PIECING
A method for sewing many units together in a row. You feed your pinned pieces of fabric under the needle, one right after the other without cutting the threads in between each set. It comes out like a chain and then you cut the threads between all the sets when you are done.

SQUARE-UP
To lie out, measure and trim all the sides of a project (block or a quilt top) so that it is square.

TOP-STITCH
To sew a row of stitches close to a seam so that the stitches are seen on the top and bottom of the fabric.

UGLY FABRIC
Any fabric that you bought at one point thinking you would like it and since then have decided you do not like it.

Metric Conversion Chart

Inches to Millimeters and Centimeters

Inches	MM	CM
1/8	3	.3
1/4	6	.6
3/8	10	1.0
1/2	13	1.3
5/8	16	1.6
3/4	19	1.9
7/8	22	2.2
1	25	2.5
1- 1/4	32	3.2
1- 1/2	38	3.8
1- 3/4	44	4.4
2	51	5.1
3	76	7.6
4	102	10.2
5	127	12.7
6	152	15.2
7	178	17.8
8	203	20.3
9	229	22.9
10	254	25.4
11	279	27.9
12	305	30.5

Yards to Meters

Yards	Meters
1/8	.11
1/4	.23
3/8	.34
1/2	.46
5/8	.57
3/4	.69
7/8	.80
1	.91
2	1.83
3	2.74
4	3.66
5	4.57
6	5.79
7	6.40
8	7.32
9	8.23
10	9.14

Index

Index